8 -
и

Homebuyers
Beware

Homebuyers Beware

Who's Ripping You Off Now?—What You Must Know About the New Rules of Mortgage and Credit

Carolyn Warren

Vice President, Publisher: Tim Moore
Associate Publisher and Director of Marketing: Amy Neidlinger
Executive Editor: Jim Boyd
Editorial Assistant: Myesha Graham
Development Editor: Russ Hall
Operations Manager: Gina Kanouse
Senior Marketing Manager: Julie Phifer
Publicity Manager: Laura Czaja
Assistant Marketing Manager: Megan Colvin
Cover Designer: Chuti Prasertsith
Managing Editor: Kristy Hart
Project Editor: Betsy Harris
Copy Editor: Karen Annett
Proofreader: Water Crest Publishing
Indexer: Lisa Stumpf
Senior Compositor: Gloria Schurick
Manufacturing Buyer: Dan Uhrig

© 2010 by Carolyn Warren
Published by Pearson Education, Inc.
Publishing as FT Press
Upper Saddle River, New Jersey 07458

This book is sold with the understanding that neither the author nor the publisher is engaged in rendering legal, accounting, or other professional services or advice by publishing this book. Each individual situation is unique. Thus, if legal or financial advice or other expert assistance is required in a specific situation, the services of a competent professional should be sought to ensure that the situation has been evaluated carefully and appropriately. The author and the publisher disclaim any liability, loss, or risk resulting directly or indirectly, from the use or application of any of the contents of this book.

FT Press offers excellent discounts on this book when ordered in quantity for bulk purchases or special sales. For more information, please contact U.S. Corporate and Government Sales, 1-800-382-3419, corpsales@pearsontechgroup.com. For sales outside the U.S., please contact International Sales at international@pearson.com.

Company and product names mentioned herein are the trademarks or registered trademarks of their respective owners.

Printed in the United States of America

First Printing October 2009

ISBN-10: 0-13-702016-3
ISBN-13: 978-0-13-702016-4

Pearson Education LTD.
Pearson Education Australia PTY, Limited.
Pearson Education Singapore, Pte. Ltd.
Pearson Education North Asia, Ltd.
Pearson Education Canada, Ltd.
Pearson Educación de Mexico, S.A. de C.V.
Pearson Education—Japan
Pearson Education Malaysia, Pte. Ltd.

Library of Congress Cataloging-in-Publication Data

Warren, Carolyn, 1950-

  Homebuyers beware : who's ripping you off now?—what you must know about the new rules of mortgage and credit / Carolyn Warren.

    p. cm.

  ISBN 978-0-13-702016-4 (hbk. : alk. paper) 1. Mortgage loans—United States. 2. Credit ratings—United States. 3. House buying—United States. I. Title.

  HG2040.5.U5W357 2010

  332.7'22—dc22

                             2009027598

Wendy L. Smith and Brian T. Smith,
thank you for your enthusiastic support
of my writing projects.

Contents

Acknowledgments

To all the good folks who read my first book, and especially to those who e-mailed me messages of appreciation and encouragement, a big thank you. And thank you in advance to all the shrewd and intelligent people who take the time to enhance their education about credit and home financing by reading this one.

To my brilliant literary agent, John Willig, president of Literary Services, Inc., who had the instinct and foresight for the timing of this book, I express my appreciation.

A special thank you to Jim Boyd, executive editor at FT Press, for taking on this project. And to the entire team, I express my gratitude: the marketing group for writing the title; Chuti Prasertsith for designing the cover; the development editor Russ Hall for his attention to detail; Julie Phifer for managing the digital marketing; Laura Czaja for managing public relations; Betsy Harris and Karen Annett for their editorial expertise, and to everyone else who helped make this book a success.

To the extraordinary people who gave me encouragement and provided suggestions for this book, I celebrate your unique talents and skills: Rick Cashman and Ed O'Connor (Advanced Funding Solutions, Inc.), Kathleen Gunovick (talented writer), Kimberly Peterson (talented home decorator), Wendy Smith (talented Realtor), Emily Vermilyea, and Saundra White (talented loan processors).

Chapter 20, "Why You Need Agent Representation," could not have been written without the input of great professionals in the field of real estate, the hard-working agents who are outstanding advocates for their clients (in alphabetical order by last name):

Heath Coker, Cape Group Real Estate, www.CapeGroup.com

Marc Cormier, ReMax Allegiance, www.Help34.com

Sam DeBord, RE/MAX, www.SeattleHome.com

Michael A. Eaves, Long & Foster Real Estate, Inc., www.MikeEaves.infre.com

Ross Ellis, Halstead Property, www.Halstead.com

Jamie Flournoy, Assist-2-Sell, www.SellingSanJoseHomes.com

Patrick Flynn, Keller Williams, www.kw.com

Gary Herbst, Buyers Edge Realty,
www.BuyersEdgeRealty.com

Daniel Merrion, City Point Realty, www.CityPointRealty.com

Judy Moses, Pathway Home Realty Group,
www.PathwayHome.com

Wendy Smith, Coldwell Banker Danforth,
www.CBDanforth.com

Darren Sukenik, Prudential Douglass Elliman,
www.DarrenSukenik.com

Paul Vranas, Vranas Properties, Inc.,
www.VranasProperties.com

Don Williams and Leslie Spennato, Prudential Georgia Realty,
www.DonWilliams1.com

This wouldn't be complete without acknowledging Steve Harrison, www.RTIR.com, and Brendon Bruchard, www.Lifes GoldenTicket.com, for teaching me their marketing secrets (highly recommended for all authors).

Last but first in my heart, I want to thank my husband Brandon for tolerating my long hours on the computer and for taking me out to eat or ordering in pizza when I was too frazzled to cook; and to all my wonderful family for their unconditional love and support.

About the Author

Carolyn Warren has been a mortgage industry insider for more than twelve years. She worked in both retail and wholesale lending for some of the largest national lenders including Full Spectrum Lending/Countrywide Home Loans, Ameriquest, Green Tree Financial/Conseco, and First Franklin wholesale lending.

Carolyn Warren is the author of the best-selling *Mortgage Rip-Offs and Money Savers*, a book that became *The Washington Post*'s August 2008 Book Club pick-of-the-month and earned reviews in publications ranging from *The Boston Globe* to the *Orange County Register*, *The Seattle Times* to the *Arizona Republic* and *San Diego Union-Tribune*. She has appeared on many radio talk shows, including Bob Brinker's national *Money Talk* and *The Gil Rose Show* in San Francisco.

Currently, she is working as a broker/banker and is the owner of two Web sites, www.AskCarolynWarren.com and www.Mortgage-Helper.com. She lives in Seattle with her husband and Himalayan cat.

Introduction: New Rip-Offs

The loan shark who bragged about making $40,000 in commissions off of one homeowner contacted me again. Last time we met, we enjoyed filet mignon at an upscale restaurant, Daniel's Broiler, overlooking Lake Washington, and he divulged to me his secret for overpricing loans, which I revealed to the world in *Mortgage Rip-Offs and Money Savers*. What would he have to say to me now? I wondered if he'd be angry.

I couldn't help but shudder at the sound of his voice over the phone, and yet, I couldn't resist the invitation to meet with him again. I just had to know how his "story" ended. Had he reached his goal of retiring rich while still a young man?

He suggested we get together at Starbucks, quite a step down from the elegant steak house we dined at before, but I didn't care. For me, it was all about the insider information.

So with a tall skinny DoubleShot in hand, I settled comfortably into a mocha-hued leather chair to hear what Mr. Big Commissions had to say. He wasted no time getting right to the point.

"What if I could show you how people can pay off their 30-year mortgage in seven to ten years *without* refinancing and *without* changing their current lifestyle—would you be interested?" he asked.

"Yes, of course," I said.

"And if I could also show you how people can leverage themselves to have a million dollars or more in savings in the time they'd normally pay off their mortgage, would that be even better?"

"Yes, of course."

"Great. Then if I show you this and it makes sense to you, is there any reason why you and I couldn't do business together?"

"Good job asking a preclosing question," I said, recognizing the sales tactic. I couldn't help but smile. This was going to be good. "So what is it?"

He chuckled and sat a little taller in his chair, like he was pleased at the rapport he was building. "You see how easy that was? Everybody says yes at that point. And here's the beautiful thing: With this program, you generate passive income. Agents are making 30 grand a month—for part-time work."

Passive income? Money coming in with no more work required? At that point, I knew it had to be some kind of multilevel marketing plan where the people at the top of the pyramid got paid on the sales their recruits made; before I could ask, he whipped out the latest edition of *Broker-Banker Magazine* and showed me the feature article endorsing the equity acceleration program. According to the article, the founders of the company were all about helping America get out of debt. The publisher of the magazine proclaimed, "This is the real deal."

It was a doozy, all right—one of those "too good to be true" things. But it looked so good on paper, people were eating it up, sales were booming, and anyone who passed a super simple test had the opportunity to make a ton of money.

And when money pours in, you know what happens next. Copycats decide they want a piece of the action, and they start up businesses with essentially the same program, but with a different name and logo.

Soon after, in came the e-mails from folks asking me about equity acceleration programs. Sure enough, the sales agents were busy recruiting other sales agents and the word was spreading. The homeowners contacting me now wanted to know whether or not this program was legitimate. (My response is in Chapter 27, "Deception Exposed.") People now are less naive, asking more questions than they did a few years back, before jumping into something.

That is a good thing.

Ever since the mortgage meltdown of 2007, the world of credit, homebuying, refinancing, and equity management has changed. Over 250 lenders died a slow and painful death, or in some cases, a sudden crash and burn. Tens of thousands of loan officers were out the door and even more were struggling to hang on and ride out the storm, hoping for better days ahead. Others moved on to new schemes, looking to make just as much money, only this time, with less work required.

Ethical loan officers working in the best interests of their clients did what they could to be a light in their spheres of influence, but the economic crash was a behemoth involving too many players in high places, too big to control.

👎 Bad Practice

Taking a risky loan, paying too much, and glossing over the details of your contract.

👍 Good Practice

Understanding the terms of your loan and choosing low-risk financing.

Teaser rates, deceptive "pick-a-payment" loans that gobbled up home equity like a hungry hippo, giant prepayment penalties, loans for people with no verifiable income, and other insanities led to the mortgage meltdown of 2007–2008. On multiple occasions, I tried to stop borrowers from signing toxic loans, but they would have none of it.

One evening, I called a nurse to warn her that her loan was obscenely priced and to explain how she could get a fair deal. I was incensed that a greedy loan shark would take advantage of a woman who had served in a hospital, caring for the sick, for 25 years, and I wanted to help. But instead of being grateful, she responded by filing a complaint against me for meddling in her business.

All that is history now...so has the craziness ended? Or has the absurdity simply reinvented itself for the current conventional market? Take a clue from these recent true stories...

👎 Bad Practice

Paying for nonsense fees you don't understand that serve no purpose except to pad profits.

👍 Good Practice

Feeling confident about your financing because you work with a loan officer who is your advocate, who explains everything clearly, and who treats you right.

- A banker surprises her homebuyer with an $11,000 "Discount Fee" that did not appear on the original Good Faith Estimate. When the homebuyer asks what the new fee is for, the bank's loan officer replies, "I don't put the Discount Fee on the Good Faith Estimate so as not to confuse people." Then she slides into some rhetoric about how she thinks God led the homebuyer into her office—or should I say, her spider web?

- An escrow company charges $100 to transport loan documents back to the lender by Fed Ex *and* a $40 courier fee to transport the loan documents. So are the documents going by Fed Ex or by courier? And since when does Fed Ex charge a hundred bucks for an envelope with 50 sheets of paper? When I call the president of the escrow company about this nonsense, he says, "Those fees don't go to Fed Ex or to a courier; they're just for our own profit."

  "So they're bogus fees?" I ask.

  "They're just there for our profit. We use a courier for about half our loans, but charge it on all," he confesses. Evidently, he doesn't think the $650 escrow fee and the $85 doc prep fee are enough profit, so he fabricates two more fees—from the president's mouth straight to my ears.

- A self-proclaimed mortgage expert tells loan officers not to worry about the decline in business. At his seminar, he'll coach them on how to make 20 grand on a single loan, "as easy as shooting fish in a barrel." He boasts of making 10 million dollars personally. To back up his claim of having the "financial secret," one of his protégés testifies that he now makes "six times what I used to get on a loan, while working just 35 hours a week." This is not a pitch for subprime loans; this guru's borrowers have 720+ credit scores.

Don't be deceived: The lust for money is alive and growing like a ravenous monster. New so-called anti-predatory laws lull people into a stupor, convincing them that all the bad loans have died like a fabled sea dragon—but that's not true. Many of these laws are doing more harm than good, and bad advice disguised as helpful tips are circulating around the Internet faster than a nasty virus.

I know all too well. I'm in the trenches, in the thick of what's going on, helping people avoid scams, ploys, and tricks—and get the best financing possible.

My Credentials

After working in subprime lending for Ameriquest, GreenTree Financial, and Full Spectrum Lending/Countrywide, I spent seven years working for a squeaky clean full-service mortgage broker in Seattle. During this time, I worked simultaneously as a mobile loan signer, which made me privy to the loan terms of dozens of additional lenders.

Then to advance my career, I accepted a position as an account executive with First Franklin, a wholesale mortgage company that lent money to mortgage brokers all across America. This made me privy to what went on behind closed doors: underwriting exceptions that turned denied loans into approvals, bribes, fraudulent loan applications, advertising strategies and ploys, "off sheet" rate pricing for "special clients," lavish parties designed to bring in more business, and some shocking confessions made by certain individuals in management. First Franklin is no longer in business.

Now I'm back in touch with Main Street America, helping good folks buy houses and refinance. (For more information, see my Web site, www.AskCarolynWarren.com.) As a homebuyer's advocate, I am telling you that it is possible to get a fantastic deal and save tens of thousands of dollars on your mortgage—but only if you avoid the financial land mines. That is what this book is all about: exposing the latest and greatest deceptions and helping people save a king's ransom on their home financing.

What's Coming Up

Chapter 1 exposes lies and shows you how to get the cheapest loan ever.

When you apply for a mortgage or refinance, the first thing the lender wants to know is your credit rating. Now like never before, credit is king. So, Chapters 2–3 provide updated information on the credit requirements, and how to raise your score faster than you ever thought possible.

Chapter 4 reveals the secret to getting bad credit deleted from your credit profile, including an actual letter I wrote (that you may copy) to get a collection account removed, pronto.

Chapter 5 is a practical five-step plan for people who want to own their own home.

Chapter 6 is for all the good folks who had a foreclosure or short sale and now want to buy a home again.

Chapter 7 is important for every citizen: how to protect yourself from crooks who want to steal your good name. Since ID theft is the fastest-growing crime in America, it's time to get tough and outsmart the hoodlums.

Chapters 8–19 reveal insider tips that can save you thousands of dollars when you buy a home or refinance. Avoid bogus junk fees and get the lowest rate with this information.

Chapter 20 is a unique perspective on real estate agents. It answers such questions as, "Is my real estate agent making a killing, at my expense?" and "Will I get a better deal if I call the agent on the for sale sign?" This information is for both buyers and sellers.

Chapters 21–23 separate truth from fiction and show you how to avoid being ripped off when doing a refinance. Warning: If you have equity in your home, you're a sitting duck for greedy loan sharks.

Chapter 24 covers special loans and situations, such as getting a Home Equity Line of Credit, a Reverse Mortgage, a Kiddie Condo for your collegiate, and more.

Chapters 25–28 will blow your socks off, as they expose the newest scams and ploys designed to take money out of your pocket and set the loan officer laughing all the way to the bank.

Chapter 29 reveals what goes on behind the scenes with appraisals and why the new HVCC law has loan officers fuming.

Chapter 30 is a wrap-up, a personal message, and resource information.

Feel free to browse the chapter titles and subheads and skip around to the topics that interest you most. When you're finished reading, I'd love to hear from you. You can send me an e-mail via my Web site at www.AskCarolynWarren.com.

Easy Reference Guide: Terms to Know

If you come across an unfamiliar mortgage term, use this page for an easy explanation.

APR, Annual Percentage Rate

A figure that includes both the interest rate and some of the up-front fees, calculated as if the up-front fees were amortized over the life of the loan. There is disagreement among lenders as to which fees should be included in the APR calculation; therefore, two lenders with the exact same loan could show different APR figures.

AU, automated underwriting or DU, desktop underwriting

The computerized software program that approves or denies loan applications. Sometimes the program neither approves nor denies, but refers it "with caution" to a human underwriter. AU or DU approval is the first step; a human underwriter reviews the loan file before final approval and before loan documents are drawn up for signing.

Discount Fee

Interest paid up front to buy down the interest rate charged on your loan Note, the money you are borrowing. Also called points (see the next page).

DTI, debt-to-income ratio

All the debts listed on your credit report plus your proposed house payment in relation to your gross (pretax) income. This ratio is used to determine what loan size you qualify for.

escrow

1. An escrow account is money set aside for paying property taxes and insurance.

2. An escrow company is a neutral middle party used in some states for closing the loan and handling the disbursement of funds. (Other states use an attorney or title rep. instead.)

FHA loan, Federal Housing Administration

Commonly called the first-time homebuyer's loan (although, you don't have to be a first-time homebuyer to use it) because the down payment is only 3.5 percent.

GFE, Good Faith Estimate

A form that lists the terms and all the costs of your loan.

loan officer, loan consultant, mortgage consultant

These and other titles are used interchangeably by employees of banks, brokers, direct lenders, and credit unions.

LTV, loan-to-value ratio

Your loan amount in relation to the price or value of the property. This ratio is used as one of the factors determining your interest rate.

neg. am., negative amortization

A loan where the payment does not cover the entire interest due; therefore, the balance goes up every month. These loans became popular right before the mortgage meltdown. These loans are also called pick-a-payment loans because you get to choose whether or not to make the fully amortized payment each month.

Origination Fee

A fee paid up front to the lender. Also called points. If you opt not to pay this fee, then you will have a higher interest rate on your loan.

par rate

The lowest rate of the day (rates change daily and sometimes midday as well) that you can get without paying extra to buy down the rate.

points

Percentage points. One point is 1 percent of the loan amount. For example, one point on a $100,000 loan is $1,000. Paying points up front in your closing costs is done to get a lower interest rate over the life of the loan. It is income tax deductible (consult with a CPA for individual advice).

TIL, Truth-in-Lending form

The form that gives additional information about your financing, including whether or not there is a prepayment penalty and the total cost of your financing.

underwriter

A person who approves or denies loan applications.

YSP, Yield Spread Premium, back-end commission

Money paid by the wholesale lender to the mortgage broker after the loan closes when the interest rate is higher than par rate.

1

Getting the World's Cheapest Loan

When Leanne applied for a home loan, she didn't expect to get the runaround, a pack of lies, the bait and switch, a condescending tone, and imbecilic answers to her straightforward questions. She didn't expect to be charged meaningless fees that served no purpose except to pad company profits at her expense. She didn't expect to engage in a royal battle just for asking what the Yield Spread Premium was on her loan. All she wanted was a low interest rate and a fair deal. Her credit scores were over 740, and she had a good income, so how hard should that be?

Leanne didn't realize that state lawmakers were scurrying around passing insidious laws with deceptive titles like "antipredatory" that were actually making it more difficult for good, tax-paying citizens like herself to get a cheap mortgage.

If you, like Leanne, just want a low rate and a fair deal, you'll benefit from knowing what happened to her—and how she ended up getting the world's cheapest loan.

Save Time and Money by Learning from This True Story

After a long day at work, Leanne was relaxing on the sofa with Puddles curled up beside her when she heard the TV newsman announce that home prices had dropped again. She thought, "I should stop throwing away my money on rent and buy my own home." The more she thought about it, the better she liked the idea of getting out of her boring beige apartment and into a home where she could paint with color and use her own decorating ideas. It would be great to have a yard of her own where she could grow tulips and maybe some tomatoes. Suddenly, she felt happy. She was going to stop supporting the landlord and invest in *her own* real estate.

So Leanne opened her laptop to see what interest rates were being offered and what her payment might be. Unwittingly, she clicked on an ad that said lenders would compete to get your business. At the time, it seemed like a good plan. What she didn't realize was that it was a lead-generation service that sold your private information to lenders, who then passed on the cost to you.

The next day, her e-mail flooded with offers for loans. She fished out her yellow pad to take notes.

👎 Bad Practice

Trusting a lead-generation service to shop your loan for you.

👍 Good Practice

Skipping the middleman by contacting mortgage brokers or banks on your own. That way, you avoid having your credit report pulled too many times and you avoid the extra cost.

Lender A said, "No Origination Fee!" However, Leanne noticed it was replaced with a Discount Fee, which was also one percentage point. The headline was a deceptive marketing ploy. How annoying.

Lender B said, "Lowest rate!" And it was true: It did have the lowest interest rate. But there was an Origination Fee and a Discount Fee totaling 3 percent. Did they think she was going to be seduced by the rate and ignore the up-front costs? That was insulting.

Lender C said, "If they quote you a rate, but don't include the APR (Annual Percentage Rate), they are in violation of federal law. Stay away from shady lenders like that. Always ask what the APR is."

So she called Lender B with the lowest rate who said, "The APR is not what you're charged on your Loan Note. The APR is a combination of the interest rate and some of the fees. The problem is that different lenders include different fees in the calculation of the APR, and all it takes is one click of the mouse to take fees out of the APR. You don't compare APRs to find the cheapest loan."

That was eye-opening, and this news made her distrust these lenders, who were now calling her cell phone every five minutes. She wished she hadn't clicked on that ad. She called her sister and asked who they used when they bought their house. It was a local company she'd never heard of, but her sister said, "This guy got us a wholesale rate. You've gotta call him." So Leanne did, and she learned he was a mortgage broker who shops the wholesale divisions of banks to find cheap loans.

The mortgage broker said, "I hope you're not calling a long list of lenders asking what the interest rate is—because verbal quotes mean nothing. In fact, I can guarantee you that if you go with the person who gives you the lowest quote on the phone, you're going with the biggest liar. Some dishonest loan officers knowingly underquote. You'll get into your loan process and then they'll say, 'Sorry, rates went up.' And there's nothing you can do about that. They never intended you to have that lowball, impossible interest rate. It was just a way to get you in the door."

"What should I do then?" she asked.

"You have to get a written Good Faith Estimate. That will show you the terms of your loan, the rate, all the fees and costs, and your monthly payment," the broker said. Then he offered to e-mail Leanne a Good Faith Estimate.

👎 Bad Practice

Calling around to get meaningless verbal quotes on a loan. No one can be held to a verbal quote.

👍 Good Practice

Asking for a Good Faith Estimate so you can review all the terms of your loan offer and see the interest rate, payment, and closing costs.

Now Leanne felt like she was getting somewhere. It made sense to get something in writing. Still, she wanted to do another comparison, so she called a large mortgage lender with a good reputation.

The loan officer said, "I'd be happy to give you a Good Faith Estimate, but first I need to get your social security number and $35 so I can pull your credit report."

"I'd like to see the Good Faith Estimate first," said Leanne. She didn't want to shell out $35 and have her credit pulled when she wasn't sure if this would be a good offer.

The loan officer said, "Oh, I can't give you that until I run your credit report. I can take Visa or MasterCard for the deposit; which do you prefer?"

"My credit is perfect. There should be no problem. Can I just see the Good Faith Estimate first?"

"I'm sorry; it doesn't work that way. I have no way of being able to give you an accurate quote without seeing your credit scores. This is the way it works," said the loan officer.

"Not for everyone. I just got a Good Faith Estimate from a mortgage broker, and he didn't pull my credit," Leanne said. "I'm not about to give out my social security number when I don't even know what all the fees are. I need to compare loan offers first."

👎 Bad Practice

Divulging your social security number and paying a credit report fee before you've reviewed and approved the Good Faith Estimate.

👍 Good Practice

Getting your Good Faith Estimate before depositing money with the lender.

Now she was annoyed. Even though she explained her credit was excellent, she couldn't even get a decent quote without having her personal credit report pulled? It didn't seem right.

Before hanging up, Leanne asked, "By the way, what is the Yield Spread Premium for that interest rate you gave me?"

"Oh, the Yield Spread Premium? Why do you ask? Um, that's not something you pay for, so, um, it really doesn't matter to you, um, you don't have to concern yourself with that. Ha-ha. Anyway, it won't be determined until we get to the HUD-1, you know, the closing." ← LIES

With that pack of lies hurled at her, Leanne decided to stop in at a bank. Maybe she'd be treated better if she went in person.

The banker was all smiley and friendly, and she handed Leanne some brochures and a booklet, along with the Good Faith Estimate. But then she pointed out that in order to get this interest rate, which she said was discounted by a quarter percent, Leanne would need to switch her checking and savings account over to this bank.

Leanne noticed there was no Yield Spread Premium disclosed, so she asked.

The banker said, "We don't have Yield Spread Premium. That's how we, as a bank, save you money!"

What kind of balderdash is that? All lenders, including banks, can sell interest rates higher than the par rate. Being a bank doesn't automatically equal saving money on a mortgage. Leanne learned that banks don't call their overage a "Yield Spread Premium" so they can claim they don't have it. Even more frustrating is that the lawmakers say only the brokers, not the banks, have to reveal their overage or back-end commission. The laws are working against the homeowner who wants transparency with their financing. The law eliminates a level playing field between banker and broker, making it harder for good citizens to compare loan offers and get the cheapest financing. What are these lawmakers thinking? Are there behind-the-scenes incentives going on that motivate them to give big banks preferential treatment?

Leanne wanted to work with the mortgage broker, but she decided she needed to put personal feelings aside and go with the cheapest Good Faith Estimate, so she set an appointment to go back to the bank to sign the paperwork and get started. She wasn't wild about the idea of switching her checking and savings accounts, but figured it would be worth it to get the .25 lower rate. Boy, she was in for a surprise.

The banker had an "updated" Good Faith Estimate and had a hefty Discount Fee that wasn't there before. "What's this new fee?" she asked. "It wasn't there before."

"As a matter of course, I don't put that on the initial Good Faith Estimate so as not to confuse people," said the banker. "But don't worry, it's standard. Please sign and date here."

"This is bait and switch!" Leanne said this loudly so the people standing in line for the bank tellers turned to look. Then she stood up, snatched the Good Faith Estimate off the banker's desk, and stomped out, ignoring the banker's protests behind her.

"Talk to my buns because it's the last time you'll see them," she muttered as she pushed through the revolving door.

The next day, Leanne conducted another Internet search, and that's when she stumbled upon my Web site. I responded to her e-mail message, and that's how I became privy to what was going on. After our consultation, Leanne went back to the mortgage broker, the one who clued her in on getting a Good Faith Estimate in the first place and completed the preapproval. Now she was ready to go house shopping.

Leanne found a newly built home that was perfect. The builder said he'd throw in $12,000 worth of extra amenities if she used his preferred loan officer. No problem, thought Leanne.

The preferred loan officer ran her credit and provided a Good Faith Estimate. He said, "This is a discount rate that you get with us because we are approved with this fine, quality builder."

But something was wrong. The so-called discount rate was .5 higher than every other Good Faith Estimate. And there were more fees, too. So to get the so-called free builder incentive, she had to pay more for her loan every month for the life of her loan? That was a bad deal in the long run!

About that time, Leanne learned that she needed to have her own buyer's agent represent her; and that if she didn't, she would almost surely pay more than needed. She decided to walk out of that rat's nest and start over. She contacted an experienced Realtor to represent her.

(handwritten margin note: MAKE SURE BANK LIST GFE ~~int~~ Dis. FEEON)

ad Practice

to a builder to purchase a home without having your own
or represent you.

👍 Good Practice

Letting your buyer's agent, a licensed Realtor, present your offer to
the builder and negotiate the terms for you, including your right to
get independent financing without giving up advertised perks.

To hasten the story, Leanne's Realtor helped her find a charming
house that had more character and a larger yard than the new construction property she'd looked at earlier. She negotiated a good Purchase Agreement, and, finally, the loan process was under way. She
cooperated fully with the mortgage broker, getting him all necessary
paperwork in a timely manner. I reviewed her Good Faith Estimate
and confirmed that all the fees were legitimate and fair. While we
were discussing her options about buying down the interest rate, I
mentioned that the loan Origination Fee is income tax deductible.
That's when a brilliant idea shot out of the heavens like a bolt of
lightning.

"Why not ask your mortgage broker to take out the two lender
fees (the underwriting fee and the processing fee) and include them
as part of the Origination Fee instead? That way, you will get to tax
deduct those as well," I said.

"What a fantastic idea! I can use all the tax deductions I can get!"
she said.

The strategy worked like a charm.

So, Leanne got the lowest possible interest rate, no bogus junk
fees, and even turned the mandatory lender fees into a tax deduction.

"You know, you've got the cheapest loan in the world," said her
mortgage broker at closing.

Once the move was being rep...ted that she and Puddles were supre...ly happ...ll good to be investing in her own home and for ...ining ...advant... aving a mortgage rather than renting ...Leanne painted he...val... utter cream yellow and planted tulips in her ...

Make Your Experience Easier, Smoother, and Better

With the knowledge you'll receive in this book, there's no reason for you to go through the exhausting process Leanne did. Homebuying can be easy, smooth, and stress-free when you apply these three principles:

1. Compare Good Faith Estimates and select a good loan officer right up front.
2. Use the (free) services of a good real estate agent to represent you.
3. Keep in touch with your loan officer throughout the process, and consider rolling the lender fees into tax deductible, up-front percentage points.

Coming Up Next

If anything in this story wasn't totally clear, the upcoming chapters will explain everything. And as you read in the Introduction, feel free to skip around to the topics that interest you. But first, we need to look at the number-one concern lenders have: your credit. With the new risk-based pricing, no one can gloss over the credit requirements.

2

What's New with Credit

"Send me your UGLY loans," said the subject line in an e-mail dated April 4, 2007.

Inside was this:

> Your loan is so UGLY, even the paper shredder is scared of it.
>
> Your loan is so UGLY, it scared the stitching outta Frankenstein.
>
> Your loan is so UGLY, the janitors use it to keep away the rats.

There were funny cartoon figures illustrating each line. Then at the bottom, it said, "Don't get stuck with an UGLY LOAN! Call <our company, toll-free number> today!"

Those were the times when late payments, collection accounts, and low credit scores were as welcome as Krispy Kremes. No matter what was on a credit report, the correct response was, "No problem." And the competition for those ugly loans was fierce.

First, one lender announced you could get a zero-down loan with a 600 score, then a brash competitor announced they'd take a 590 score. "Look at all the extra business we'll bring in with those ten extra credit points!" announced an excited sales manager to his staff.

One month later, another competitor rolled out zero-down loans with a 580 score. It was like two corner gas stations in a bidding war. Lower and lower the requirements went, each company trying to pick up more of the market share, competing to be in the top five of all subprime lenders—er, excuse me, nonconforming lenders.

Not wanting to offend anyone by calling them subprime, the loan officers replaced the term *subprime* with the kinder, gentler *nonconforming*. They even made it sound like it was an advantage. Using a confidential tone as if letting them in on an insider secret, they told their customers, "You can get approved with us because we don't go by those super strict rules used by the stuffy banks. Being a nonconforming lender, we don't conform to their rules."

"That's good!" said the happy borrowers, who were so onboard with skipping the stuffy bank rules.

Getting more loans approved and beating the competition for loan volume knew no end. One morning when I was working as a retail loan officer for GreenTree Financial, we loan officers entered the conference room, lattés in hand, and slipped into our seats for the weekly staff meeting. Little did we know that our manager was in his corner office seething, livid with rage, because our office came in third that month. But we were soon to find out.

He busted through the conference room doorway like an out-of-control freight train. His red face popped out of his starched, white dress shirt like an overripe tomato ready to burst as he paced around the room and shouted, "I will not come out in third place next month! Is that clear?" The tirade went on for several hours, and we got the message that no loan applicant was to be denied.

This was about more than money. His overripe ego was suffering the loss of a bet with another manager who came out in second place for the month.

"This will not happen again! If you value your job here, you will close more loans! Is that NOT CLEAR TO ANYONE?" he roared.

👎 Bad Practice

Lenders being too lax with their credit requirements. This put many of them out of business.

Approving "everybody," knowing that some loans would go bad. This is no longer acceptable.

👍 Good Practice

Lenders being diligent to make sure borrowers are creditworthy.

This doesn't mean you must have perfect credit, but you do have to show some creditworthiness to get approved.

The next month, I boarded a plane and flew from Seattle to Spokane, Washington, met the borrowers in the airport, signed their papers, and flew back home an hour later. Our office paid for my airfare. That's how important it was to squeeze every possible refinance into the month in order to beat the competition. We could not waste time waiting for an escrow company in Eastern Washington to overnight signed documents back to Seattle.

Back then, beating the competition and getting every loan closed was the name of the game. How times have changed.

Today, applications get turned down.

Today, credit is king.

Are You Getting Ripped Off By Your Own Credit Score?

When you apply for a home loan—whether it's to purchase a property or to refinance—the first thing that gets checked is your credit score. I'll tell you about the rare exception later, but 99 percent of the time, if you don't pass the creditworthiness test right up front, your loan application will not get in front of an underwriter's eyes. (Underwriters are the people who approve and deny loans.) You might say that if you have a low score, you're setting yourself up to get ripped off because you'll pay more or be denied altogether.

1. Without an acceptable credit score, your loan application will be stopped by the computer before a human underwriter even looks at it.

    The first step to getting your loan approved is automated underwriting (AU), or desktop underwriting (DU). The loan officer—or the loan officer's teammate, the loan processor—inputs your application information into the computer. The program automatically pulls your credit report and analyzes all the information on your application, lickety-split. If your credit score is too low, the computer will spit out the dreaded words, "Declined/Ineligible"; and unless you've got a way of getting an exception, your dream of buying a home ends there. It's back to working on your credit for you.

Once the computer underwriting program has accepted your loan application, there is another way your credit score affects your mortgage.

2. Without a premium credit score, you will pay a higher interest rate.

In subprime lending, it has always been true that the lower your score, the higher your interest rate. That was risk-based lending. For people with good credit, the loans were a pass/fail system. If your credit score was 620, you qualified for a good conventional loan and having a score of 800 made no difference in your interest rate. That is no longer the case. It's as outdated as avocado-colored appliances. It used to be that the FHA first-time homebuyer loan and loan for U.S. Veterans did not go by credit score at all. That is no longer the case. It's as outmoded as harvest gold shag carpet. Risk-based pricing has come to all mortgage loans, for all credit types, and lenders have charts showing how much more you will pay for your interest rate, based on your credit score and loan-to-value ratio. (Your down payment or the equity you have in your home determines the loan-to-value ratio. The bigger the down payment or the more equity you have, the better it is for the lender's security. And the better it is for your interest rate.) More details about that in the next chapter, but first, we need to understand how the credit scoring system works.

👎 Bad Practice

Using 620 as a benchmark for getting the best interest rate is an outdated standard. It resulted in too many foreclosed properties.

👍 Good Practice

720 is now the minimum credit score desired. Some loan programs require 740 to get the best pricing. Therefore, the new goal is to achieve a score of at least 740.

How Lenders Rate Credit

Originally, credit scoring was called "bankruptcy scoring." Lenders wanted to evaluate their risk in loaning money, so the loan officer had a paper scorecard to evaluate a person's chances of going into bankruptcy. The loan officer asked the applicant questions, checked boxes with a ballpoint pen, and then added up the score at the bottom of the page. So, yes, credit scoring is older than the personal computer.

In the late 1980s, the Fair Isaac Corporation (FICO) created a complex mathematical algorithm by analyzing millions of credit histories and using about 40 variables. This numeric scoring system enables consistent, impartial evaluation of loan requests. It proved to be astonishingly accurate in predicting the risk of granting credit—most of the time.

Thanks to Fannie Mae and Freddie Mac endorsing its use for evaluating mortgage loan applications, in 1996, computerized credit scoring became the standard for loan approval. And now there are three credit reporting agencies, or credit bureaus: Equifax, Experian, and TransUnion. Although there are additional credit bureaus (credit reporting agencies) now, those are still The Big Three.

Frustrating the public, for years the credit bureaus kept credit scores strictly hush-hush. A few renegade loan officers who disagreed with the policy secretly told their customers what their credit scores were and what score they needed, but for the most part, no one knew their score. Then in April 2001, Equifax made credit reports with a credit score available online to the public. On December 4, 2003, President Bush signed into law the right of every person to receive one free credit report per year. But that doesn't mean the score has to be provided with it.

Your credit score is a number between about 350 and 850 that grades you on your creditworthiness. The credit score is an index of risk. It is an unbiased indicator of whether you will repay a loan on time. The score changes as new information is added to or deleted from your credit file. On the day your credit report is pulled, the computer instantly tabulates your score by the information on hand at that moment. The score is based on all the credit-related data, not just negative data. Your established patterns of credit and payment correspond to the likelihood that you will make your payments on time or "as agreed" in the future.

When the credit bureaus began raking in the dough by selling scores and other information, Web site owners spied an opportunity.

Beware of Bogus Credit Scores

If you have a television or computer, you've seen the ads for a free credit score. Such a deal! We're all curious about our scores, and why pay when you can get it for free? But wait.

Those free scores are probably not the same score your loan officer gets when he pulls your credit for a mortgage approval. I can't tell you how many upset and disappointed folks I've talked with who were shocked and disgusted when I told them their actual score.

"What?!" they shrieked. "Last week, my score was 720. What do you mean it's 654? What happened? How could it go down like that?"

"Where did you get the 720 score? Was it from a free Web site?" I asked.

"Yes, is that a problem?"

"Unfortunately, it is. Your 720 score was from using a more lenient scoring system. It could have been made up by the Web site, or it could have been the scoring model used to approve people for credit cards. The requirements for getting a credit card are much more lenient than for getting a mortgage, for obvious reasons." I went on to explain that it's not unusual to see a 50- to 80-point variance. It wasn't that their score went down, it's more like the score they got was bogus, if they were counting on receiving their mortgage-risk credit score, as most people are.

These so-called free scores—that sometimes obligate you to pay subscriptions or put you on solicitation lists to buy services—are a waste of time and set you up for annoyances. If it doesn't specifically say that what you're getting is the FICO score (from the Fair Isaac Company scoring model), then it's a credit score of another breed.

> 👎 **Bad Practice**
>
> Ordering a free credit report on the Internet. The score you get from random Web sites is not the same score used by mortgage companies.

> 👍 **Good Practice**
>
> Going by the credit report your loan officer orders when you apply for preapproval. Your loan officer will tell you your score and will give you a copy of your report at closing.

10 Common Misconceptions About Credit Scoring

With credit scoring being so important in our credit system, it's time to clear up some common misunderstandings. Take a look at this list to see how many misconceptions you have and what the facts are.

10 Misconceptions Explained

1. Credit scores from the three agencies are averaged together to determine your credit score.

   False. Lenders go by the middle score of the three. However, if only two scores are used, the lower one is used.

2. Married people share a score.

   False. Every individual has his or her own score, which means every individual needs to have credit in his or her own name.

3. Carrying a balance on credit cards from month to month helps your score.

   False. Paying off your balance in full each month is a better idea because you avoid wasting money on non-tax-deductible interest.

4. It's a good idea to avoid the use of credit and pay cash for every-thing.

   False. This is a common mistake people who want to avoid paying interest make. In our society, everyone needs to have a good credit history and credit score. Without it, you'll have a hard time buying real estate. Ideally, you want a mix of credit cards, an installment loan (such as an auto loan), and a mort-gage to obtain the highest score.

5. All bad credit drops off your report after seven years.

   False. A tax lien, a judgment, and a bankruptcy may stay on your report for ten years or even longer.

6. The more credit you have, the better your score will be.

   False. Absolutely not. Too many open credit card accounts can actually hurt your score because you have the capacity to amass a lot of debt, which increases your risk as a borrower. If you have three to five credit cards, that's plenty. Don't go wild opening a dozen cards, if you haven't already done so.

7. You should close off old credit cards you don't need anymore.

   False. Don't do it! You gain points for longevity. This is cal-culated on both an individual account basis and on an average of all your accounts. When you close off old cards and give up those points, your score can go down dramatically.

8. It's okay to use only your favorite credit card.

   False. Some people who have an airline mileage credit card plan put all their purchases on it and ignore their other credit cards. But what you want to do is to use each major credit card (such as Visa and MasterCard) once every few months to keep it active for gaining points. One small $20 purchase once a quarter is sufficient, so you can still concentrate on racking up those airline mile credits.

9. Enrolling in a debt management service is a good idea if you have a lot of bills.

   False. Enrolling in a debt management service is usually a bad idea, especially if you want to get a mortgage soon. When your credit card provider posts "managed by a debt service" on your report, it looks bad—like you can't manage your own finances. Even worse, it can cause your score to drop—as many creditors report that you are not paying as agreed because they're receiving only partial payments. Then it goes on your report as if you have a long string of late payments. It's much better to be your own debt manager.

10. It's smart to apply for a loan through the Internet ads.

     False. People who do that are victims of a lead-generation system, as explained in more detail in Chapter 26, "Stop Clicking on Mortgage Ads."

How did you fare with the ten misconceptions? If you knew all ten were false, that's great.

One thing people like to know is how they rate compared with other Americans. Most people think they are above average, which is funny when you think about it—because it's mathematically impossible for the majority to be above average.

How Your Score Compares with Others'

The following table[1] shows the national distribution of FICO scores.

You can see why an average score of 700 (or better) is preferred by lenders. You can also see why having a score in the 800 range gets you respect when it comes to financing.

FICO Score	% of Population
350–499	2%
500–549	5%
550–599	8%
600–649	12%
650–699	15%
700–749	18%
750–799	27%
800+	13%

👎 Bad Practice

Having a below-average score. The average credit score is 720. A score below 500 is in the bottom 2 percent.

👍 Good Practice

Seeking to be in the top 13 percent with a score of 800+. You can get more strategies for raising your score at my Web site www.MortgageHelper.com.

Coming Up Next

Would you like to have the highly prized 800 credit score? Do you want to receive the red-carpet treatment on all your financial transactions? Strategies for raising your credit score are next.

Endnotes

1. http://www.myfico.com/CreditEducation/CreditScores.aspx, May 29, 2009.

3

Quick, Easy Ways to Raise
Your Credit Score

Do you just love supporting the fat cats on Wall Street? Do you want more of your hard-earned money going to increase their profits? No? Then you must pay attention to your credit score so you can qualify for a lower interest rate and pay less. Risk-based pricing is all about the risk to the lender: the lower the risk of lending money to you, the lower your interest rate.

Your FICO score, developed by those thoughtful Fair Isaac Corporation folks, is based on the middle score from the three main national credit reporting agencies or credit bureaus, as they're called.

The table below shows a sample for a purchase loan of $200,000 with a 20 percent down payment.

Purchase Loan of $200,000 with a 20 Percent Down Payment

Credit Score	Additional Fee You Pay to Get Par Rate
740+	0 or $0
720–739	.25% (of the loan amount) or $500
700–719	.75% or $1,500
680–699	1.5% or $3,000
660–679	2% or $4,000
620–659	3% or $6,000

Instead of paying the additional fee, you could take a higher interest rate. Either way, you pay more for having a lower credit score.

The fee chart varies daily with the daily interest rates, so your loan officer can advise you. Additionally, the fee chart varies according to how much down payment money (or equity) you have.

The crucial point is clear: You want your middle score of the three credit scores to be as high as possible. That way, you pay less interest into their coffers and keep more money for your own needs.

The following section describes nine ways to improve your rating, listed in order of quick and easy.

Nine Ways to Raise Your Score, Quick and Easy

Take control of your credit score. No need to be a victim of the credit bureaus when you can literally manipulate your score by taking some action steps. Check out the following strategies to see which ones you can take advantage of to improve your credit rating:

1. Place your name into the opt out list.

    One of the smartest things you can do, that takes only three minutes of your time, is to opt out of being solicited by credit card companies. It's maddening to think that the credit reporting agencies sell your information to companies that solicit you to open a bank card. But what's even worse than the junk filling up your mailbox is the fact that it hurts your credit score, too. If you ask the credit reporting agencies, they deny it—but then they have a vested interest in the scheme, so that's no surprise. On the other hand, credit experts—the people doing the field work of improving people's credit—say that they've observed an improvement of four to six points by getting on the opt out list. Why? Because the constant solicitation to open new credit and go into debt has been removed; and, therefore, the likelihood of that happening decreases. I'll grant you that it's not a lot of points, but when you're that close to reaching the desired score of 740, it can translate into hundreds of dollars of savings for you. The Fair Credit Reporting Act (FCRA) provides you the right to "opt out," which prevents consumer credit reporting companies from selling your credit file information to creditors (all that junk mail).

To do this, go to www.OptOutPrescreen.com. You can do it online or follow the directions on the Web site to do it by regular mail.

2. Set up auto-pay.

A young woman who lives close to the Great Lakes told me the late payments on her credit report were not her fault, and she was mad about it. She explained that she sent the payment on time; but because a blizzard blew down from the north, the mail was delayed. She thought it wasn't fair that the creditor posted her as being late because it was the blizzard's fault, not hers.

Here's another excuse I received for a late payment: "My gerbil shredded my bill." I have two words for all you people who suffer "extenuating" circumstances like bad weather and frisky pets: automatic payment.

It's perfect for everyone who has ever paid late due to being in Jamaica on vacation, or having the bill go through the washing machine in your jeans pocket. With auto-pay, you can't be late. And here's another perk: You don't have to spend a postage stamp, which means you can use that stamp to send your grandma a greeting card and make her day.

👎 Bad Practice

Letting unpaid bills pile up on your desk until right before the due date.

👍 Good Practice

Setting up auto-pay so everything gets paid on time, all the time.

3. Keep your balances below 10 percent of the limit.

This is my favorite tactic for raising a credit score by 60 points instantly. Here's how it works.

Your credit score is calculated at the moment your credit report is pulled. It's not calculated once a month or on a periodic schedule. Your electronic credit file is there collecting data without a score. Then when a lender pulls your credit, the computer slips it into one of 14 grading curves called score-cards, and then uses about 40 components to calculate your score. One of those components—an extremely important one—is your balance-to-limit ratio, meaning what you owe versus how much you're allowed to borrow. If your balance is $5,000 and your limit is $5,000, then your balance-to-limit ratio is 100 percent. That's bad for your credit score.

Here's an insider tip that not many people know...

The second most influential factor in calculating your credit score is your revolving utilization—both individual and aggregate. Wow, what does that mean? I'll explain.

If the balance on your credit card is near or up to the allowable limit, you get docked massive points. If the balance is 50 percent of the allowable limit, you get docked points, but not as much as if you're up to 90 percent. The lower your balance is in relation to your limit, the better. The best is having a balance of no more than 10 percent of the limit. That calculation for your Visa card is an individual calculation, and it is made for each card you have. But in addition, a calculation is made on the sum of all your balances in relation to all your available credit. That is the "aggregate calculation." Both individual and aggregate calculations are used in credit scoring.

🖓 Bad Practice

Carrying high balances on credit cards, wasting money on non-tax-deductible high interest.

👍 Good Practice

Using credit cards as a convenience and paying off the balance every month so you spend no money on non-tax-deductible interest.

The following example shows how individual and aggregate calculation works if you have two credit cards.

Individual and Aggregate Calculation of Credit Card Balances

Discover limit: $2,000   Balance: $200   Percentage to limit: 10%

Visa limit: $2,000   Balance: $1,980   Percentage to limit: 99%

Aggregate percentage to limit: 54.5%

Analysis: Discover card percentage is good, so you gain points on that individual card score. Visa balance is much too high and will lower that individual card score severely. Aggregate balance for the two cards is too high at over 50 percent, and this will also lower your score. And this has nothing to do with the fact that you've paid both cards on time forever and always.

If you pay down the Visa card to $200, you will gain points for that individual card *and* gain additional points for the aggregate percentage. See how powerful this knowledge is?

You can literally manipulate your credit score by making sure your balance-to-limit ratios are low. If you're planning to apply for a home loan within three months, pay particular attention to this powerful strategy.

4. Cherish your long-standing accounts.

The longer you have a relationship, the more painful it is in breaking up. Think of that and you'll remember not to close out your long-standing credit cards. Even if you don't need them for purchases, you need them for credit points. When you have an active account for 36 months, you get extra "longevity points." Cherish those "friendships" and don't make the common mistake of cutting them off.

So often I've heard someone wail, "I went to work cleaning up my credit and closed off all the old accounts I don't use, and kept my one airline mileage Visa card open. My credit score went down by 40 points—what happened?!"

"You just gave up all your longevity points, that's what happened," I say. "And not only that, but now you have less available credit, so the 'aggregate percentage' I explained in #3 has also decreased. This means, your current balances in relation to your total available credit has gotten worse, because you just closed out a bunch of your available credit. You've given yourself a double whammy!"

Unfortunately, the damage is irreversible because when you open a new credit card, your score is temporarily dropped because it's unknown how you will handle that account.

Now here's the exception to the rule: If you have 17 credit cards open, that's extreme, so close off half of them. One young woman, a loan officer, told me, "I have 17 relationships." She went on to explain she had 17 credit cards open with balances. That was a bad thing. She wanted to buy a house and couldn't qualify for a good conventional loan because her score was too low, even though she paid all 17 cards on time. So when you go overboard and have too much credit, it trumps the longevity rule. Call and ask specifically to have the account "closed by consumer's request," so it doesn't look like the creditor dumped you. You'll do just fine keeping the eight best accounts open.

5. Charge something every quarter.

This goes right along with the preceding rule. You want those longevity points, but to get them, you do have to keep the account in active status. The credit card you cut up and haven't used in five years is not going to give you a single "individual card point," even though, technically, it's still open.

Use your major credit card every now and then for something you were going to buy anyway to keep it active. A couple of delicious apples grown in Washington State are enough to generate points; you don't need to execute a major purchase.

As for your favorite store card, the one you're keeping open to enjoy the occasional special sale discount, you can let that lay dormant for a year or more. You don't have to be like, "Oh, I've got to go get some designer shoes every few months so I can keep my credit score up."

👎 Bad Practice

Cutting up old credit cards, never to use them again.

👍 Good Practice

Using cards sporadically to keep the accounts in open status, thereby gaining "longevity points."

6. Say "no" to credit card enticements.

"Would you like to save 10 percent today by opening up a credit card?" How often have you heard that? It seems that every store and boutique wants the opportunity to charge you 18 percent in interest, and they're willing to offer you a discount up front to get you into their lair.

Even if you pay off the balance every month so that you pay zero interest, you should say no. The hit to your credit score for (a) opening a new account, (b) lowering the average age of all your accounts, and (c) having too much open, available credit is not worth the few bucks you'll save.

If you're young and have good credit, but you don't have a long credit history, opening a new credit card can have devastating results. Don't be a sucker for a measly 10 percent savings!

Because Sears and Victoria's Secret and Target and Shell all accept the Visa card, there's no reason to open an individual store card—and a very good reason not to.

Once you have three credit cards, that's enough, provided at least one of them is a major card such as Visa or MasterCard, because it's much more beneficial to have what's considered a major card that can be used everywhere than it is an individual store card. I recommend not opening more than three to five credit cards.

Now I can just hear someone say, "But I love my Macy's card; whenever they have a special store sale, I get a discount if I use it, and last year I got this luggage at 40 percent off, which saved me beaucoup bucks."

And I say, "I know; me, too." It's okay to have a favorite store card that saves you money. Personally, I have two Visa cards that give me valuable perks (which I use) and a Macy's card, which I use on rare occasions when I want to participate in a special sale. My credit score is over 800, so it's working for me. I'm just saying don't go overboard. Don't get a card at each of your favorite stores.

7. Avoid finance companies.

Be careful when you buy furniture or electronics with their in-store financing. Many of them use a finance company such as Beneficial Finance or American General Finance. These finance companies cater to people who cannot get financing anywhere else; hence, the name "hard money lender." Because they serve this niche, the credit bureaus suspect you are hard up if you do business with them and slightly dock your score accordingly.

8. Use your HELOC to pay off excessive credit card debt.

If you already have a Home Equity Line of Credit, you can use it to bring down your high credit card balances and, thereby, improve your score. The new FICO 08 software doesn't subtract points for having a maxed-out Home Equity Line of Credit like the old credit scoring model did. (Don't use this information as an excuse to overspend on your Home Equity Line of Credit. And don't go out and open one just to pay down credit cards because it may torpedo your chances of getting the best refinance.)

9. Build a mix of credit accounts.

This last one is primarily for young people who haven't established much credit yet. If you have only credit cards and nothing else on your report, your score won't be as high as it would be if you also had an "installment loan." An installment loan is a loan with set payments and a set ending date, such as student loans or an auto loan. If you've never had an installment loan, the next time you're going to buy a vehicle, opt for financing rather than paying cash. However, if you're getting ready to buy a house, don't make the mistake of taking an auto loan just beforehand. That's a common mistake that puts a person's debt-to-income ratio too high for the home they desire.

If You Have No Credit History

If you're young or new to the country or rebuilding your credit after a bankruptcy, the best way to get started is to open a savings account with a bank or credit union that offers secured credit cards. Deposit $500 or more and ask for a secured credit card. The card limit will be the amount you have in savings. Use the card minimally each month and pay off the entire balance each time you receive a statement. At the end of six months, you can convert the secured card into a standard card and have the limit raised.

Another way to establish credit quickly is to become an authorized user on a family member's account. I recommend this option only for a parent and child where the parent maintains control over the use of the card.

If you need a vehicle, using auto financing will add an installment loan to your credit file and benefit your rating.

After six months of using credit, you will have a score. I've seen people go from no score to a 700+ score in six months.

> **Bad Practice**
>
> Having no credit in your own name.

> **Good Practice**
>
> Every individual needs to take responsibility for creating a strong credit file. Being married to someone with good credit does not help *your* credit, as each person's score is individually calculated.

Get More Respect with an 800 Score

Here's something that happened to me, true story...

I'm sitting in the office of a finance manager at an auto dealership buying my new car. He offers me 7.5 percent interest. My jaw drops open.

"My credit score is over 800. I think I deserve a better interest rate than that," I say. I sink back into my seat and fold my arms to send a message with my body language.

He shifts in his chair and buries his nose back into his computer screen while he mumbles, "Oh, let me check on that."

He pretends to do a double-check and then swivels back in my direction with a big, toothy smile. "You're right. Let's lower your rate by 2 percent," he says.

So there you have it. You get instant respect and pay less when you have a high score.

So far, the tips for getting a good score have been what I call preventive and maintenance. But what if you've already got some late pays and collections that drag down your score?

Don't worry, there's hope ahead. Get to work cleaning up your credit today, and don't you dare let that monster, Procrastination, waylay you from getting to your goals.

Coming Up Next

If you need to get aggressive to overcome some mistakes of the past, Chapter 4, "Aggressive, Innovative Ways to Fix Credit," is for you. Some of the things I say might upset some people, but I can't worry about that. These strategies work.

If your credit is already perfect, you can skip ahead as you won't need this info.

4

Aggressive, Innovative Ways to Fix Credit

Friends were coming for dinner, and my husband decided to be helpful by getting rid of a stack of papers I had out on the kitchen counter. Unbeknown to me, he swooped everything up and stashed it on top of the refrigerator. He thinks that's a great storage place because no one under six-feet-two can touch anything that's up there.

So we have a lovely dinner party, and three weeks later I finally get around to standing on a chair to clean on top of the refrigerator. That's when I discover that my Visa bill has been rotting away unnoticed; and as of that very day, I am 31 days late.

"What's this?" I shriek, wild-eyed with horror.

For me, the Queen of Credit, to be past the 30-day mark and get a "late pay" on my credit report is totally unacceptable. I fly off the chair like a bat out of you-know-where, yelling, "Why did *SOMEONE* put my Visa bill up high where I can't see it?!"

Because I cannot tolerate a ding on my credit, there's only one thing to do. Call the Visa company and ask them not to report me late.

"Can they do that?" some people might ask. After all, they've read that a true and factual late payment cannot be altered. That would be lying and illegal, right?

No, wrong.

Here's the reality—the insider information I never see written up on credit bureau or government Web sites or in so-called helpful articles about credit. Late payments *may*—not *must*—be reported to the credit reporting agencies (credit bureaus). I'll explain.

The Visa company owns my payment history information for their account. If they want to report that payment history information to all three credit bureaus, or to just one bureau, or to none at all—that's their choice. There is no law that requires Visa to report my pay history to all—or even to any—of the credit bureaus. And if someone at the Visa company wants to give me grace and not report my one-day late payment, that is their prerogative. It's not illegal and it's not considered lying to forgive someone and call it good. It is allowed. If someone is 60 days late, they can choose to forgive it and call it good. It's up to Visa because it's Visa's account.

So I call up the toll-free number and ask to talk with a supervisor about my billing statement.

"I've been a customer of Visa for many years," I say. The guy looks up my record and quotes back the exact number of years.

I continue, "You can see from your records that I've never been late. I am your ideal customer." I pause for a second. Come to think of it, maybe I'm not their ideal customer because I don't carry a balance from month to month, so they never make their outrageous interest profit on me. Oh well, never mind that. I go on.

"I just now discovered that my Visa bill got missed this month. It was hiding on top of my refrigerator, and I didn't know it. I would like to pay today by phone, but I would like some grace and not have a late payment reported to the credit bureaus. My credit is really important to me, and I don't want my perfect credit messed up by this one-time mistake."

"Just a minute, let me see," he says. So I sit and wait. When he comes back on the line, he has good news. "No problem, Mrs. Warren. We'll take your payment now, and we will not report the account as late."

So I make payment; and sure enough, when I check my credit report later, I confirm that no late payment was reported.

I smile. I am happy with my Visa card company. And they have just strengthened their business relationship with a valued customer.

Must DO

Innovative Method #1:
Use Charm to Get a Goodwill Agreement

Any time you have an "uncharacteristic" derogatory item on your credit report, you have an opportunity to receive grace and have it deleted. Even if it's more than one day late. Even if it's already been reported to the credit bureaus. Even if it's a collection or charge-off.

One afternoon, I was talking with a hard-working woman who farms in rural Washington State. Much to her surprise, she received a letter from out of the blue saying her collection account was past due and needed to be paid immediately. It was for some ancient catalog order, and she wasn't aware she owed money. I happened to be at her home enjoying a slice of homemade apple pie when the letter came, so I coached her on what to do; less than 30 minutes later, the collection account had vanished off her record. You, too, can do what she did. Here's how:

1. Call the company and say, "I would like to speak with a supervisor who has the authority to make exceptions to your rules." Make sure you go a level above the customer service representatives.

2. Explain that you had no idea there was a past-due account on your record. Be friendly and charming. Explain that your credit rating is very important to you and that you are in the habit of paying everyone on time. They can look at your credit report and see this is true. Obviously, don't say this if it's not true. If you have multiple accounts past due, skip this strategy and use another one.

3. Say you will be happy to pay what you owe, *but first*, you need to have an agreement that they will give you grace for this "one-time, uncharacteristic mistake." That's the magic phrase. Tell them you don't want your credit rating ruined over one charge-off you were not made aware of. Now let me make an important point here…

   Everyone has feelings, including the supervisor you're talking to. Don't say, "YOU never sent me a bill." That's offensive and annoying and won't win you any points. This is a goodwill request, so you want to be amicable. Instead say, "I know it's not your fault, personally, but I never received proper notice. Someone's computer must have messed up or whatever." See the difference and how the second statement is more likely to gain a goodwill agreement? If you're dealing with the collection department of the original creditor and not an outside collection agency, you can even add, "I always like shopping at your store; you have the best such and such. I'm surprised this payment snafu happened, but I'm sure we can straighten it out now." Set yourself up as being on the same team, working out the problem together. Don't set yourself up as a pit-bull lawyer coming against them, ready to tear them apart. One woman told me she couldn't get the cooperation of her creditor to remove her late payment, and I found out later it was because she swore at the representative, so don't make that mistake.

In addition, if it's a very old late payment that has been reported as being a collection or charge-off, it is very important that you don't make payment until after you've received a written confirmation that your payment will be considered "paid in full, as agreed." You can get confirmation by e-mail, fax, or regular mail; but make sure you get it in writing. Otherwise, if they "forget" or don't bother to send you confirmation after they have your cash, you'll have no proof that you paid in full per your agreement. Uncharacteristic mistakes can be—and are—forgiven. And why not? If a person has years of perfect pay history, why should a one-time mistake ruin their high score and their chances of getting the best financing? It's common sense and common courtesy.

👎 **Bad Practice**

Passively accepting a late payment on your credit when you have a pattern of paying everything on time.

👍 **Good Practice**

Asking the creditor to forgive your late payment to keep it off or delete it from your record. This is legal for the creditor to do, and it's a good business decision to retain their good customers.

Innovative Method #2: Demand the Removal of Old Collections and Interest Charges

A gentleman named Don asked for my help in getting an old collection from a men's clothier off of his credit report. I wrote a letter for him that got immediate results. The company was not only happy—they were eager to tell the credit bureaus to delete the collection from Don's credit file. They also apologized and said they hoped he would continue shopping at their fine store.

👎 **Bad Practice**

Lying to the credit bureaus. *For the record: I do not endorse lying.*

👍 **Good Practice**

Getting the cooperation of the creditor who owns your credit information to help you clean up your credit in a manner that is legal and ethical.

Now that's what I call a satisfactory resolution. Please note that there was no lying involved. I do not endorse lying. Here are the steps I took in writing a successful letter.

Seven Steps for Writing a Successful Letter of Demand

These steps are like a recipe or a road map for writing a letter that gets positive results.

1. I found the company's Web site by typing the name into the Google search. Then I clicked on Contact Us to find the phone number and mailing address.

2. I called and asked for the name of the supervisor in charge of the Customer Relations department. I asked for the correct spelling of that person's name and confirmed the mailing

address. They were happy to assist and even gave me the department number to include in the address.

3. I wrote the letter addressed to the specific person in charge of customer relations. Always take this step if you want first-class success. Don't be lazy and write "Dear Sir or Madam." A letter written to a generic human like that might be tossed aside and ignored. Think of it this way: Which letter will you open first? The letter written to you by name or the letter written to "Resident"?

4. I was specific but short in telling the story of the nonpayment. And in doing so, I politely let them know it was their fault.

5. I reminded them that under the Fair Debt Collection Protection Act, I have the right to request and receive an explanation of a balance due *before* being reported as late—and that they were in violation of the law by reporting the collection to the bureaus before proper notification was given.

6. I reminded them the Fair Credit Report Act states I have the right to receive the following documents as proof of debt validation:

   a. A copy of my agreement with the company

   b. A copy of this agreement with my signature showing I agreed to the terms of the credit account

   c. A copy of the complete payment history of the account, so that the exact amount of the debt can be determined and agreed upon by both parties

7. I proposed a reasonable resolution, which was that Don would pay the original amount owned, minus late fees and interest charges, after he received a letter of confirmation stating that (a) the collection was in error and requested to be deleted from his credit file, and that (b) the original balance minus the late fees would be considered "paid as agreed/paid in full."

Then, just to ensure a satisfactory response, I ended the letter with a zinger. Instead of telling you what it was, I'll let you see it for yourself as you read the following letter. I've taken out the name of the store because they cooperated fully, and I don't want to disparage them.

Actual Letter of Demand to a Men's Clothier

Dear Mr. <Name of Customer Relations Supervisor>,

For many years, I have shopped at <Store Name>, and I have always appreciated the customer service and quality of clothing.

Early this year, I purchased $596 worth of clothes, which is not unusual for me. But on this particular day, the sales representative pushed me to apply for a <Store Name> credit card in order to save another 10%. He was insistent, so I agreed, and I didn't think any more about it.

Just recently when I was reviewing my credit report, I was stunned to find an entry for a charge-off from the <Store Name> for $596, plus a hefty collection fee, to total $893. Because I always pay my bills on time and have A+ credit, this came as a shock! Thinking back, I realized I never received a bill from the new <Store Name> credit card. Furthermore, I never received a letter notifying me the account was late, nor did I receive a phone call. In fact, I received no notice at all! (If I had, I would have promptly paid.)

Under the **Fair Debt Collection Protection Act**, I have the right to request and receive an explanation of a balance due *before I am reported as being late*. I was never notified of this past due bill or collection; therefore, <Store Name> is in violation of the law by reporting this collection account to the credit bureaus.

Furthermore, the **Fair Credit Reporting Act** states I have the right to receive the following documents as proof of debt validation:

1. A copy of my agreement with <Store Name>
2. A copy of this agreement with *my signature* showing I agreed to the terms of the credit account
3. A copy of the <u>complete payment history</u> on my account, so that the *exact amount of the debt can be determined and agreed upon by me*

Because I have not received the aforementioned legal documentation, I have the right to sue your company for $1,000 in damages for each violation of the FCRA. Mr. <Name of Supervisor>, I <u>do not want to sue</u>. All I want is to pay my original debt of $596 and to have you send a letter to the credit bureaus you report to (and a copy to myself) stating the collection was an error and to delete this negative entry from my credit report.

I'm sure you will agree this is fair and reasonable for both of us. You receive your money owed and retain a valued customer, and I restore my otherwise perfect credit. I will be happy to send a check promptly as soon as I receive a letter of confirmation from you stating the following:

1. The collection is in error and is requested to be deleted from my credit file.
2. The amount of $596 will be considered "paid as agreed/paid in full."

I look forward to your prompt reply. I would like to continue to be a regular customer at <Store Name>, and I will feel good about doing so once we get this matter cleared up.

Sincerely,

Aggressive Method #3: Insist They Stand by Their Original Agreement

Once your collection is paid off, it's more difficult to get the creditor to agree to remove it from your credit report. Before you've paid it off, they want some money. The collection reps get paid commissions or bonuses based on the money they collect, so there's a lot of incentive to bargain. The mistake most people make is when the collector says, "Sure, I'll remove the collection from your report when I receive payment." They take the representative at his or her word without getting it in writing. Look at it this way: Joe (or Jane) the collector couldn't care less about you, your circumstances, or your credit. Joe is on the phone for one reason only—to do his job and make money for himself. When he collects money from past due accounts, he gets paid, too. So that's his mission. He will do what he has to do, which might include agreeing on a settlement and even agreeing on removing the derogatory account from your credit report. I used to visit collection companies every week to negotiate settlements and do business, so I happen to know something about what goes on there behind the locked doors between the customer lobby and the reps.

👎 Bad Practice

Making payment on a settlement after receiving only a verbal agreement by someone who isn't even using his real name.

👍 Good Practice

Getting your agreement in writing first and then making payment.

Sometimes collection agencies have incentives and contests as a way of keeping their reps dialing and talking to people who don't want to hear from them. It's a tough job, so the bonuses and prizes help keep them dialing for dollars, hour after hour.

Understandably, there is still a high rate of turnover in the collection business. A few months of calling people who yell and cry on the phone, and many of them are ready to quit. Collection companies are always looking for new hires to replace the people who got burned out or who acquired better jobs.

Here's another piece of interesting information. The reps use fake names to protect their identities. Why? Because they don't need some loose cannon who didn't appreciate their phone call looking them up at home and threatening their life. So Joe the collector might call himself Jack Daniels or Jack Nicholas or Jack Abbott, depending on his favorite pastime. Some of them have a good bit of fun picking their pseudonyms. When I worked in subprime lending, I visited one large collection agency where they all took on names of celebrities, but that's another story.

The important point is, the typical collection rep doesn't stay at the collection agency very long, and he or she uses a fake name. So if you failed to get your verbal agreement in writing, you have a challenge on your hands. You'll never do that again, right? But for now, you've got to deal with it.

Call up the collection company and explain that you're not happy because you kept your side of the bargain by paying them money, but they have not yet kept their side of the bargain by deleting the collection from the credit bureau.

👎 Bad Practice

Giving out your bank account information to make payment by automatic deduction. Once you authorize them to get their long, bony fingers into your account, there's no telling how much will be withdrawn. And good luck trying to fix it after your money is gone!

👍 Good Practice

Paying a collector by money order to keep your bank account information 100 percent private.

At this point, they'll probably say they don't do that because it's their general policy; however, you know they make exceptions because they did for you.

So you politely explain that you know they don't usually do that, but in your case, your rep—Jack or Joe or Jason or whatever his name was—promised you that when they received their money, they would extend you the favor of deleting the collection from your credit file. You explain that is the only way you would have agreed to pay, *of course!*—because as everyone knows, paying an old collection hurts your score and makes it go down when the "Date of Last Activity" is updated on your credit report. Therefore, you would never have paid it if you hadn't also received an agreement—a verbal contract—to have the account removed from your file. And you checked your credit report recently and were totally shocked and dismayed to find out that their end of the bargain hadn't been kept yet—and you want that corrected right now, today, because you aren't going to stop pestering them about it until it's done. After all, a deal is a deal, and an agreement is an agreement, verbal or written. Period.

Keep asking for a higher authority, a supervisor in charge, a company president, even the CEO, if necessary, and repeating your story until you get cooperation. Sometimes, one collection rep passes the phone to his friend sitting next to him, and he pretends to be a manager. Happens all the time, so don't be intimidated about asking for a higher authority.

And then next time, don't trust Joe the collector's verbal agreement because you aren't talking to someone who's using his real name, and he probably won't even be working there anymore by the time you have to follow up. Get your agreements in writing, right up front, before any cash exchanges hands.

For more in-depth, insider information about improving your credit, please see my Web site, www.MortgageHelper.com, and click on Credit Scoring.

👎 Bad Practice

Trying to manage your credit and finances without sufficient knowledge.

👍 Good Practice

Acquiring knowledge through information at www.Mortgage-Helper.com.

Coming Up Next

If your credit isn't good enough to qualify for an approval right now…if you don't have a down payment saved yet…if you want to buy a house someday, but for some reason, can't do so now, my five-step plan coming up next is for you.

And even if your credit is good, you might pick up an idea there that will be beneficial, so have a look and have fun with these steps.

5

Five-Step Plan for People Working Toward Buying a Home

If your credit is so ugly it scares Frankenstein, and you don't have the cash for a large down payment, then hold on to hope and set your eyes on your goal. Although you might not qualify today, you can get there in 6 to 12 months, so take heart and get busy on my five-step plan.

Five Fun, Easy Steps to Home Ownership

How can a secret strategy used by a top salesman who earns $250,000 a year help you achieve your dream of buying a home? When you copy the ideas and actions of successful people, you, too, will become successful in achieving your goals. Here are the tips that have been proven to work:

1. Collect pictures of houses you'd like to own that are *realistic for your income.* Either print out photos from online or pick up a free real estate for sale magazine at the grocery store. Choose a few houses that are in your actual price range. Post them on a bulletin board or refrigerator or mirror where you'll see them and be inspired on a daily basis. Write out, "I will buy my own home by <select a date 6 to 12 months in advance>."

    This is to create a strong, concrete visual of your goal. This step is not childish; it is important. Sales trainers who get paid thousands of dollars to coach sales personnel and entrepreneurs on how to achieve amazing goals teach them to create bulletin boards, lists, and other visuals. Having something you can see every day is a part of the process that leads to success. It is a strategy that's employed by high achievers.

A goal that is not written down is not a true goal, it is a dream—and dreams fade away. You need more than a dream—you need a solid goal. So if you want to turn your desire into reality, then create a visual for yourself. It's been proven to work. But that's just the first step, so let's continue.

👎 Bad Practice

Having a fuzzy idea about becoming a homeowner someday.

👍 Good Practice

Creating a strong, concrete visual of possible homes, along with your target date for home ownership.

2. Put a sticker on your credit cards and your checkbook. I'll explain how this works. When you're out at the mall, you're not in front of your house photos, and it's all too easy to get caught up in the shopping moment and overspend or buy things that are not necessities. It happens all the time to a lot of people. So here's what you do: You put a reminder on your credit cards and checkbook to help you pull in the reins. What you're doing is reprogramming your brain to create a new life habit, and you're going to use something as simple as a sticker to do it.

One idea is to get a blank label, write the letter *H* on it, and cut it out. You put the *H* on all your credit cards and checkbook. The *H* stands for house. It reminds you that you're saving toward a house and that the sacrifice you're making now in passing up that outfit, that handbag, those golf clubs is going to be worth it in the end. Twenty dollars saved is like 25 dollars earned because you don't pay taxes on it. Twenty dollars here, 100 dollars there, it all adds up over six months. You'll be surprised. In fact, every time you pass up a purchase you were going to make, write it down in a log; that way, you can see for yourself how much money you're saving.

Another idea is to use a Post-It note and write the word *house* on it and stick it on your credit cards and checkbook. This sounds simplistic, but it produces impressive results. One afternoon I was having lunch with a top-producing account executive who pulled in an income of a quarter-million dollars a year.

"What's your secret to success?" I asked. He pulled out his wallet and showed me a shiny gold sticker, a small round circle of gold.

He explained, "Every day, I pull out my wallet and look at this gold circle. It reminds me that I'm 'going for the gold.' When my day is done and it's time to go home, I pull it out and look at the gold sticker. Then I make one more sales call before I go home. That's what has made me the top producer at my company. This gold sticker and one extra call a day."

And that's where I got the idea for step 2 in my plan. It's all about taking better control of your spending, cutting back on your spending, and saving more money.

👎 Bad Practice

Using money to buy little things to cheer yourself up, forgetting about your bigger goal.

👍 Good Practice

Taking control of your finances through visual reminders.

3. Order your credit report through the U.S. mail from each of the three credit reporting agencies. Federal law mandates that you have the right to a free credit report each year. Get it and analyze it. Then, because you've ordered it through the mail, you can effectively dispute any errors or any bad credit that should have expired from your report. Send your disputes through the mail also. Don't be lazy and do it online because you might need a paper trail later, if you're disputing derogatory items.

   In short, this step is to clean up your credit report as much as humanly possible. Don't discount this step by saying it's hopeless, or it will take a long time. I've seen plenty of people's credit reports improve by 80 to 100 points in less than a year. No one is hopeless unless they decide they want to be that way.

And remember, time is on your side. The older derogatory items get, the less they hurt your score. At the same time, the longer you establish positive credit, the more it helps your score. For more information about credit score improvement, see my Web site, www.MortgageHelper.com.

4. Stash cash. I adore the squirrels that run through my backyard scouring for food. Sometimes, I toss out peanuts for them. In the spring, they grab the peanut and eat it; but in the fall when the days are getting short and cold, they grab the peanut and run off to save it. I watch them dig a hole, bury the nut, and then pack the soil back on top, so the jays can't steal it. The squirrels are savers, and I admire that about them.

   When I wanted to buy my first house, my husband and I were young and didn't have any extra money to make saving possible. So I found a second job working as a grocery checker in the evenings, and I stashed every check into a separate savings account. In a year, we had our down payment. When you want a house badly enough, you do what it takes to save up cash.

   Now for the fifth and last step.

5. Read your way into a house. That's right—read! Buy books, check out books from the library, and download e-books about home buying and credit improvement. That might sound strange at first, but the reality is, if you educate yourself about credit and home buying, if you continue to keep it at the forefront of your mind, if you *stoke the fires of passion* for becoming a homeowner—you will achieve that dream.

   Don't ever discount the power of reading for achieving an important goal. You show me one person who says they want to buy a house but complains that they can't because of their credit; and then you show me one person who says they want to buy a house in spite of the fact that their credit is all shot to hell at the moment, but who reads at least one book a month—and I'll show you who's still paying the landlord and who's unlocking the door to his own home 12 months from now.

   Here's a secret. You can pay a personal coach $3,000 to $10,000 or even more to help you achieve your personal goals. Or, you can spend $150 on books and gain essentially the same information. It's fantastic! Books inspire, educate, and empower. Read and implement—and then repeat. Do it every month and you'll be led straight into your own piece of real estate.

   Now go back to step 1 and get started. Today.

Coming Up Next

Who among us doesn't know someone who faced foreclosure or had to short sale their property back to the bank? Please reach out to those folks and let them know it's not the end of the world. The next chapter offers inspiration, hope, and the answer to their biggest question: When can I buy a house again?

6

How to Recover from a Foreclosure or Short Sale

If you are facing or have endured a foreclosure, you have my sympathy. It's never easy, under any circumstance, to pick up and move out of a house against your wishes. In a moment, I'm going to show you how to buy a house again; but first, I want to give you a word of encouragement by saying a foreclosure is not the end of your life, your happiness, or your hope for the future. The way some people talk in their e-mails, you'd think it was the end of the universe.

If you have a foreclosure, adopt a positive perspective. You're not really losing your home. Home is where the heart is, and if you take your heart with you, you'll make a new home elsewhere.

Don't think of it like you've lost your home. Think of it like you've lost a piece of property. Big deal. What is a piece of property? Land, cement, brick, stucco, wood, glass, and so on. It's just material. It is not your flesh and blood. It is not your life. Yes, you might have created memories there, but you can take those memories with you in photographs, journals, and in your mind. You will go on to make new memories—better ones. You can buy property again in the future—perhaps an even better house than the one you had before.

One day I received an e-mail from a woman who was facing foreclosure and she had some stinging words for me. Even though she and I were complete strangers—she happened to stumble upon my Web site—she felt the need to vent her anger in my direction about her pending foreclosure.

She wrote, "I'll bet you've never gone through anything like this. I bet you don't know how hard it is to lose a home and to have to tell your kids you have to move across town to a bad neighborhood because you can't keep up with your mortgage anymore…." She went on and on, and I could tell she thought I was sitting high up in some castle impervious to pain. But that's not the case.

I do know what it's like to lose a spacious, beautiful dream house and move kids into a tiny apartment across town. I went through that—not because of a foreclosure, but because of an unfortunate divorce—but the result was the same. We lived in an upscale neighborhood called Seahurst, and I loved the house so much I told my friends I was going to live there forever. Sometimes I'd sit at one end of the living room and look out over the spaciousness and feel the gratitude for living in such a wonderful place. But all that changed.

As a result, I took my elementary-aged children and moved across town into an apartment that was so small, my daughter and I had to share a bunk bed because two beds couldn't fit into our bedroom. My kids switched schools, and they no longer lived across the street from their friends. But you know what? They survived.

We got ourselves a fluffy little kitten to grace our new home, something the children had been asking for. After a year, the kitten grew into a cat, and I was able to move my children and our kitty out of the apartment into a modest house. As we were packing, my son said something I'll never forget because his words were like a healing salve on my bruised heart.

He said, "It's going to be weird moving out of here, mom, because this is our *home*."

At that moment, I knew I'd been successful as a mother—I had made that 780-square foot apartment into a *home* for my children. It was a place where we had peace and love and happiness and hope for a brighter future.

Home is the place you share with your loved ones; it is not an address.

So if you are facing a foreclosure or have already gone through one, cheer up. It's not a tragedy like the death of a child. It's not the end of the world. It's not even the end of having a home. Make a new, albeit temporary, home. And then forge a plan to buy a house again later.

How Long After a Foreclosure or Short Sale Until You Can Buy Again?

In the era of subprime lending, you could get a mortgage one day after a foreclosure, and you still can—*if your down payment is large enough*. There are private investors who don't care one whit what's on your credit report; in fact, they don't concern themselves with looking at it. It's all about the equity in the house, so if you came into some money and can put 30 percent or more as a down payment, I have a list of 86 investors who have money to lend (available via my Website, wwwMortgageHelper.com).

On the other hand, if you're looking for a conventional loan, here are general guidelines regarding the waiting period between the foreclosure and when you can be approved for a mortgage issued by the Federal National Mortgage Association August 1, 2008.

Easy Definitions

Foreclosure: The lender initiates legal proceedings to terminate your rights to a property and to conduct a forced sale of the property.

Deed-in-lieu of foreclosure: You give the lender the Deed—the legal instrument of ownership—in exchange for canceling the debt.

Short sale: The lender agrees to sell your property for less than what you owe.

- **After a foreclosure:** 5 to 7 years
- **After a foreclosure with extenuating circumstances:** 3 to 7 years
- **After a deed-in-lieu of foreclosure:** 4 to 7 years
- **After a deed-in-lieu of foreclosure with extenuating circumstances:** 2 to 7 years
- **After a short sale:** 0 to 2 years (If you did not have a 60-day late payment, there may be no waiting period.)

Getting an Exception for Extenuating Circumstances

What constitutes an extenuating circumstance? If your interest rate went up? No. If your loan officer lied and gave you the impression you had a fixed-rate mortgage when it was really an adjustable rate mortgage—where your payments would skyrocket and become unaffordable? No. In both of those cases, you are responsible for reading the documents and making a good decision.

An acceptable extenuating circumstance is something beyond your control, such as a death in the family, a medical emergency, illness, or job loss from being laid off. If that is the case, you might get approved earlier. And that will depend partially on the individual lender and how strict the underwriter is. **Warning:** You don't want to be going from bank to bank trying to find someone who will accept your extenuating circumstance, having your credit report pulled over and over again. I recommend going to a mortgage broker who knows the wholesale account executives and underwriters; that way, the mortgage broker can call around for you without the credit pulls and without the stress to you.

The Great American Comeback

I'm going to end this chapter by saying it's not just the income-challenged folks who experience a foreclosure. Rich and famous celebrities have gone through it too.

Stars whose properties went into default are Whitney Houston and Aretha Franklin, queens of soul music; Evander Holyfield, heavyweight boxing champion; Jose Conseco, pro baseball player; and Damon Dash, cofounder of a hip-hop record empire. Scott Storch (the music producer for Beyonce, Christina Aguilera, and other stars) was living the good life with a $10-million, 10-bedroom house on Palm Island, Florida. After falling on hard times, he lost his house, his Ferrari, and his motorcycle. To top it off, he owed personal friends the sum of $170,000.[1]

Celebrities are known for their roller-coaster lives. One minute they're on top of the world, and the next, they're at the bottom of the heap. But they don't stay down for long. They do what they have to do, make a comeback, and then rise to stardom again.

America loves a good comeback. So be inspired and create a comeback of your own. Your future can be better than your past. So you lost a plot of land with a house on it. So what? You're still alive! Pick yourself up, fix your credit, rebuild your reputation, and buy again.

You read how I went from living in my dream house down to a tiny apartment. Now I'm living in another dream house that's even better than my first dream house. That's what I want for you, too—so don't you dare give up hope. Make a stellar comeback. Show the world you won't stay down for long.

Coming Up Next

Heads up! Thieves are stealing the identity of good people and using it for their own evil deeds. Everyone you know needs to be alerted about how to protect themselves from this crime epidemic as explained in Chapter 7, "Beware of Privacy Pirates!," coming up next.

Endnotes

1. "Celebrity Foreclosures," http://www.luxist.com/photos/celebrity-foreclosures/999757/, November 3, 2008.

7

Beware of Privacy Pirates!

Can you imagine the horror? You're sitting at the kitchen table sipping hot coffee and reading the daily news when, out of the blue, there's a loud banging at the front door. It's the police—and they're looking for YOU. They bust into the room shouting your name. One of them reads you your rights while the other slaps handcuffs on your wrists. You have no idea what's going on because you haven't done anything. I mean, you might owe ten cents for the library book you returned late last week, but this?

The officer informs you you're under arrest for the murder of two women. One of the bodies was just found in the trunk of a car in Florida. Sound far-fetched? Michael Berry of Arlington, Virginia, had his identity stolen by a convicted murderer, and the story was reported in the *Washington Post* on August 6, 2003.

Identity theft is no joke. The stress and trauma caused to victims of identity theft is parallel to what is experienced by victims of a violent crime, according to the "Identity Fraud Survey Report" by Javelin/Better Business Bureau.

Having your bank account hijacked and your good name ruined by imposters is too devastating to ignore. We must take aggressive steps to protect ourselves.

How to Protect Yourself from ID Rip-Off Artists

By now, we should all know not to leave credit cards and wallets in unlocked desk drawers and other handy places because it's common for cards to be stolen by people we know—coworkers, friends, and even family members. Disgusting, but true. Extensive surveys have shown that people who know you will take your cash and your plastic when temptation dances in front of them.

One woman I spoke with loaned her credit card to a needy person in her church to buy some clothes, and the person ran up the card to its maximum of $9,000 and then disappeared. You're probably rolling your eyes at that story because you know better than to lend your card to anyone. So instead of stating the obvious, I'll attempt to offer ideas you haven't already heard elsewhere because it's time to get aggressive against these scoundrels.

Five Proactive Steps to Avoid Being a Victim of ID Theft

You're not living in your grandmother's world; it's not okay to leave your door unlocked when you're gone. In fact, it's not okay to leave out any of your personal information where it's vulnerable to being ripped off. You must safeguard your name and credit in today's world. Use the following steps as a checklist to protect yourself:

1. Have your initials, not your first and middle names, put on your checks. For example, instead of Victor C. Newman, put V.C. Newman. That way, if someone steals your checkbook, they will not know how to sign your first name, but your bank will know.

2. Put a work phone number on your checks rather than a home phone number. If you have a P.O. Box, put that on your checks rather than a home address. And never print your Social Security number on your checks.

3. Don't sign the back of your credit cards because it gives away your signature to crooks. Instead, write "Photo ID required." It's unlikely a thief would have your picture ID, and if they did, it's even more unlikely the thief would look like you.

4. Avoid writing out your account number on the "For" line when you write checks to pay your credit card bill. You never know what type of person might be handling your check processing. Instead, just write the last four numbers of your account; that's all the credit card company really needs.

5. Place the contents of your wallet on a photocopy machine— driver's license, credit cards, important phone numbers, the works. Photocopy both front and back sides. Write the toll-free numbers for each card next to it. Then keep the photocopies locked in your home safe or in your bank safety deposit box, where you'll have it in case your wallet is lost or stolen. While you're at it, make a photocopy of your passport and carry that with you next time you travel internationally. We've all heard horror stories about pickpockets in other countries.

👎 Bad Practice

Signing the back of your credit cards so a rip-off artist will know exactly how to forge your signature.

👍 Good Practice

Writing "Photo ID required" on your credit cards as a safety guard against fruadulent use of your credit.

Five Steps You Must Take If Your ID Is Stolen

If your driver's license, passport, or credit card is stolen, don't wait to take action. One of the problems in getting this horrendous crime under control is that too many people don't report it fast enough. Fact: 39% of the ID theft victims did not report the crime for five years, giving the crooks a lot of free play.

Five Steps for ID Theft Victims

If your ID is stolen, time is paramount for protecting yourself. Here are the steps to take:

1. File a police report immediately in the jurisdiction where the theft took place. Keep a copy of the report and case number.

   Credit card companies, your bank, and the insurance company might ask you to reference the report to verify the crime. You'll also need a copy of the report to remove any false information from your credit reports.

2. Contact your credit card company to close out the account and get a replacement card with a new account number.

   If you made photocopies and kept the toll-free numbers, as recommended previously, then you're prepared for immediate action.

3. Call the fraud units of the three credit reporting bureaus.

   Report the theft. An account reported as lost or stolen does not hurt your credit score. Also, add a statement to your report that requests that they contact you to verify future credit applications before they're made. This is to protect you from a thief opening up new accounts in your name. If you do this immediately, you can stop the crooks dead in their tracks.

**Contact Information for the Three Credit
Reporting Bureaus and the
Social Security Fraud Line**

**Equifax Credit Information Services/
Consumer Fraud Division**
P.O. Box 105496
Atlanta, GA 30348-5496
(800) 997-2493

Experian
P.O. Box 2104
Allen, TX 75013-2104
(888) 397-3742

TransUnion Fraud Victim Assistance Department
P.O. Box 390
Springfield, PA 19064-0390
(800) 680-7289

Social Security Administration/Fraud Line
(800) 269-0271

---

4. Keep a log with dates of all conversations with authorities and financial institutions.

5. Report the theft to the Federal Trade Commission. Although the FTC does not have authority to bring criminal cases, they are a clearinghouse for complaints by victims of identity theft, and they assist victims by providing information to help resolve problems that result from the theft.

**Consumer Response Center
Federal Trade Commission**
600 Pennsylvania Ave. NW
Washington, D.C. 20580
(877) 382-4357, or TDD (202) 326-2502
www.ftc.gov/ftc/complaint.htm

What to Do If Your ID Is Lost

If you misplace your credit card, there's no need to panic and cancel your account. What if you shut down your card, issue a stolen alert on your credit report, open up a new card with a new number—and then discover your credit card was in your other jeans pocket all along?

When I couldn't find my Visa card, I called the customer service number and found out where my last transaction was. It was at a restaurant I dined at two days prior. I then called the restaurant and learned they had my card locked in their safe. I retrieved my card, no feathers ruffled.

If a call doesn't locate your card, ask the creditor to put a freeze on your card. That way, no one can make a purchase until you call back and unfreeze the card. This will keep it secure from fraudulent charges while you hunt for it.

Unfortunately, a few companies won't give you the courtesy of placing a freeze on your card, so if you can't locate it, you might have to go ahead and report it as "lost or stolen." But beware: Once you report your card as stolen, you cannot undo it, even if you find your card two seconds later.

You Can't Be Too Careful

When you safeguard your good name and identity, you safeguard your ability to qualify for all the best financing—on your home, auto, or anything else. If you'd like to know more about the exploding white-collar crime of ID theft and how the devious crooks pull off their schemes, pick up a copy of Bob Sullivan's *Your Evil Twin: Behind the Identity Theft Epidemic*.

Coming Up Next

Before you make an offer on a house, read Chapter 8, "Don't Buy a House Until You Read This." It reveals winning strategies for getting your offer accepted, even if you're competing with other homebuyers.

8

Don't Buy a House Until You Read This

One key to home-buying success is getting the seller to say yes. Whether you're presenting an offer below asking price to a private party, or competing with other bidders on a bank-owned foreclosure, you have to persuade the seller to say yes to your offer. Let's begin with a true story about a married couple who were defeated time and again, but stumbled upon a secret, and then had instant success.

Andy and Kim were eager to quit renting and instead to buy their first house. When prices dropped in Northern California, it seemed like their opportunity had come. Their real estate agent showed them a vacant, foreclosed home they liked, so they made an offer. They were beat by someone else. They tried a second time, and were beat again. They thought "third time's the charm" and optimistically made another offer. They were beat out again.

On the fourth home they bid on, the bank was asking $149,000. Andy and Kim offered $170,000—a full $21,000 more than the asking price. After being beat out on their last three attempts, they thought they'd go really high this time.

Andy and Kim waited in suspense for ten days and ten sleepless nights to get their acceptance. Finally, the answer came.

"Sorry, someone came in with a better offer," the listing agent said. Later, they learned the buyer who beat them offered a lower price than they had.

"What does it take to get an accepted offer?" they wailed. I sympathized with them. Clearly, they needed a different strategy than the one they were using if they wanted to get their offer accepted. So what was the secret? What were their offers missing, as it wasn't about price?

Gain an Uncommon Advantage Over Your Competitors

How could they show greater strength as buyers? How could they position their offer to appear more appealing to the seller? With their real estate agent, we came up with a winning solution.

We made two changes to the presentation of their offer and hit the bull's eye. The next offer they made was instantly accepted! You can use these two strategies to give yourself an uncommon advantage as well:

1. Bulk up your earnest money deposit.

    The first change they made was to increase their earnest money deposit. The earnest money is the check you present to the seller with your offer. If you back out of the deal, the seller gets to keep your check. Putting money on the line demonstrates to the seller that your offer is "earnest" and not just a whim. When your loan is closed, the earnest money goes toward your down payment, so it's not an extra cost.

    Instead of offering one or two thousand dollars, Andy and Kim put in their entire 3.5 percent down payment (FHA loan) as their earnest deposit. Because they'd have to bring in the down payment anyway, why not present it from the get-go, impressing the seller with the financial strength they had?

Bad Practice

Presenting a promissory note for the earnest money deposit.

Good Practice

Presenting a check equal to the down payment (for an FHA loan) or a check with an amount that impresses your solidarity to the seller (for a conventional loan). Ask your real estate agent what amount that would be in your area.

2. Write a more specific, more concrete letter of approval.

The second change was to their letter of approval for financing. I scrapped the generic letter commonly used by loan officers and wrote a more specific, concrete, solid letter instead. This served in besting the competition and making the seller feel more confident in their ability to close the deal. With all the recent buyers who have gone into foreclosure, it's a great idea to let the seller know just how strong your financing is.

Following are the "before" and "after" letters. The originals were presented on company letterhead paper, but the contents are here. You can show these to your real estate agent (and recommend that your agent pick up a copy of this book) to make your own offer stronger.

Generic Letter That Brought Disappointment

Preapproval Letter for Andy and Kim Lastname
$170,000 Purchase Price
FHA Loan, 30-Year Fixed Rate

To Whom It May Concern:

Based on the credit, income, and asset information, Andy and Kim Lastname are qualified to purchase a single-family residence for the price of $170,000. This approval is for an FHA, 30-year, fixed-rate loan.

The borrower has good solid employment and meets the credit, income, and assets requirements for this loan.

The applicants' approval is subject to a valid Purchase and Sale Agreement, final verification of employment prior to closing, title commitment, and an approved appraisal of the subject property along with any other condition that the lender may require prior to closing the transaction.

Please <contact me> if you need further assistance.

Sincerely,

Carolyn Warren

Loan Officer

Now look at the difference in the new, improved letter that changed their history of getting four denials into gaining an instant acceptance.

New, Improved Letter That Brought Success

Preapproval Letter for Andy and Kim Lastname
$170,000 Purchase Price
FHA loan, 30-Year Fixed Rate

Date: *<Added current date>*

To Whom It May Concern:

Andy and Kim Lastname are qualified to purchase a single-family residence located at *<inserted property address>*.

The terms of the 30-year fixed rate, FHA loan are as follows:

Purchase Price: $170,000

Down Payment: $5,950 (3.5%)

Seller Contribution for Closing Costs: $5,950

<Terms are listed, including asking for a contribution from the seller equal to the down payment—which they readily agreed to.>

The borrowers have good solid employment and meet the credit, income, and asset requirements for the FHA loan. Andy and Kim's application, credit, income, and asset documents have been reviewed by the lender and verified as being acceptable. *<This last sentence assures the seller this is a solid preapproval, not a soft prequalification or merely an expectation.>*

Their credit scores are 752 and 770. *<Scores are good. Stating them boosts confidence.>*

Please *<contact me>* if you need further assistance.

Sincerely,

Carolyn Warren

Loan Officer

Further Explanation About the Earnest Money Deposit

To make it clear, you present your earnest money check with your purchase offer. It shows the seller you're serious and not just yanking his chain. If you back out of the deal without just cause—such as you suddenly found a house you like better—the seller gets to keep your money to repay him for taking his house off the market and possibly passing up another good offer. However, your purchase offer should include two contingencies that will allow you to get your earnest money back:

1. A contingency on financing says if your loan isn't approved, your check is returned. There is a time period, such as five days, for you to remove this contingency. This allows time for the lender to receive updated pay stubs and anything else that is needed to make your approval super solid.

2. A contingency based on an acceptable inspection report. You should hire an independent, licensed home inspector to go through the house from roof to underground crawl space to ferret out all the things that are not up to par. Attend the inspection so the expert can point and show you the details. You will then receive a written report, including photos and an explanation. If you discover the house has fatal flaws, you can back out of the deal and get your earnest money back. Or you can ask the seller to repair any of the flaws you want fixed before you take possession. Everything is open for negotiation here, and your real estate agent handles the communication back and forth for you. You might opt to have the seller credit you money in lieu of doing the repair work.

Don't skip the home inspection. Even if you're buying new construction, even if you're a handyman and can do your own repair work, even if—no exceptions. If your uncle is a contractor, I'd still get an independent inspection because what happens to your family relationship if your uncle doesn't notice something? The inspection is worth every dollar spent.

The earnest money check is held by your closing agent: your attorney, title rep., or escrow agent. At closing, it is credited toward your down payment and/or closing costs, so you will have to bring in that much less money when you sign the loan papers.

CAN IT GOES TOWARD YOUR
(EARNEST) CLOSING COST.
  MONEY

Coming Up Next

Two things home buyers want to know: Is this a good time to buy? Which type of loan is best for my personal situation? The next chapter answers these questions with a quick-and-easy read.

9

When Is the Best Time to Buy a Home?

When I was a kid, I desperately wanted one of those black Magic 8 Balls that answer all the questions of life. You held the ball in your hands, asked a yes or no question, and turned it over. Then, voila! There was your answer, in black and white. Much to my delight, I received the Magic 8 Ball for Christmas. I was mesmerized and couldn't fathom how it worked. I asked my father if he knew how it worked, and he said yes, but then he refused to tell me on the grounds that it would spoil my fun. So, my friends and I shared many moments of surprise and delight in receiving answers from the mysterious ball.

About a year later, I finally convinced my dad to tell me how it worked. As it turned out, the magic was more about a plastic wedge floating in black liquid than about a superpower. I admit, it was just a little bit of a letdown.

So now, without my Magic 8 Ball, I have to rely on clear thinking and common sense to find answers.

When Is It a Good Time to Buy?

People often ask me if it's a good time to buy a home. It's a valid question, and the answer lies in these seven questions:

1. Is your credit in order?
2. Are you free of carrying a large load of credit card and other debt?
3. Are your credit scores high enough to qualify for decent financing?

4. Do you have the income to afford a house payment, your other obligations, plus the upkeep a house requires?

5. Do you have enough money saved for a down payment, or if not, do you have gift money available for a down payment?

6. Are you ready to settle down to living in one location?

7. Are you sick and tired of paying your landlord's mortgage payment?

If you answered yes to all of the above, then it's a good time for you to buy. Skip ahead to the subhead, "The Folly of Procrastination."

If you answered no to some of the questions, let's take a closer look:

1. If your credit is not in order:

   Maybe someone else's credit is showing up on your credit report, like the man who had no children but had his brother's back child-support payments showing up as a lien on his credit; or the son with the same name as his father who had his father's late auto payments dragging down his score. Take a month or two to fix these errors so you can raise your score and get the best interest rate. The savings will be worth the effort.

Need Help Writing Dispute Letters?

I offer my services to write the most awesome, convincing dispute letters. For people who aren't trained in copywriting (convincing sales copy) or who want to save time, please see my Web site, www.AskCarolynWarren.com, for more information about my writing service or consultation service.

2. If you carry a large load of credit card and other debt:

   If your income is also high so that your debt-to-income ratio, including your new, proposed house payment does not exceed 43 percent, then there's no problem. (Calculate with your gross income, before any deductions. This is the highest number on your W2. Count the debts on your credit report, not living expenses, such as food, phone, and gasoline.) On the other hand, if your debt-to-income ratio is 50 percent or higher, get creative in knocking out some of that debt. Go on a spending diet and see how you can temporarily bring in more money. (If your debt ratio is 44 to 49 percent, your loan might get approved, depending on the overall strength of your application: credit score, assets, down payment, job stability, and so on.)

3. If your credit scores are low:

On my Web site, www.MortgageHelper.com, I offer a complete do-it-yourself system for raising your credit score.

4. If your income is already stretched to the max:

Sometimes first-time homebuyers don't consider that it costs more to maintain a house than it does to rent. In addition to the mortgage payment, you have to figure in costs you probably didn't have renting, such as garbage, possibly sewer, and periodic repair work. "Try on" your new home ownership by pretending you're living in a house. Set aside the extra money (the amount that is over what you pay for rent now) and see how that feels for a couple months. Then, you'll know whether you're stretching yourself too thin for your own comfort.

5. If you don't have enough savings or gift money available for a down payment:

The only zero-down loan is for U.S. Veterans. Everyone else will need at least 3.5 percent (of the purchase price) to put down. The seller can pay your closing costs. You'll also need two months' house payment in reserves, meaning in savings, investments, 401(k), and so on—money you can draw on to make your payment in case of emergency.

6. If you aren't ready to settle down to one location:

If your job will transfer you to another city in a year or two, you could consider turning the home into a rental property and hiring a management service to handle it for you. But if you don't want to take on that responsibility, maybe it's not the time to buy.

👎 Bad Practice

Buying a home with the idea of selling it a year later to make a profit. Values are not increasing that rapidly now.

👍 Good Practice

Choosing to buy for the long-term, at least 3 to 5 years if you are making a minimal down payment.

7. If you are sick and tired of paying your landlord's mortgage payment:

Good for you! Why pay for someone else to get richer in real estate when you could be establishing and increasing your own home equity and future security?

Don't be discouraged if you had too many no answers. Let them tell you what you need to work on, and then go for your goal. Look on the bright side: Maybe you'll find a house at a lower price when you're ready to buy.

Will You Get a Cheaper Price by Waiting?

"Will prices continue to go down? Are we at the bottom yet?" People ask this intriguing question, and because I no longer have that black Magic 8 Ball, I can only say this, "No one knows where the bottom is until prices start going up again. That applies to both house values and interest rates. We can see the bottom when we look back, but by that time, it's too late."

The Folly of Procrastination

I met a gentleman who didn't buy a house in the 1980s because he thought prices were sky-high and that he'd wait for them to come down. Look at what happened! In 1980, the median price of a home was approximately $60,000. In 2008, the median price was approximately $200,000 (according to The National Association of Realtors). And even though prices dropped in 2009, they're still nowhere near the 1980 price today.

Don't obsess over whether you could save a few bucks by waiting to buy a home. It's just as likely you will spend more by waiting, too. If the home you visit with your agent is a good match for you, then it's a good time to make an offer. This particular home is available now, not later.

Owning is better than renting in the long run. People who own their homes free and clear in their retirement years are taking Mediterranean cruises and enjoying life. By contrast, people who are renting in their retirement years are paying more than ever and are taking supplemental jobs slinging hot fries and sweeping greasy floors to try to make ends meet. It makes sense to own your refuge, your safe haven where you sleep at night, where you seek solace from the world and shelter from the storms. I'm a huge fan of home ownership.

Real estate represents personal security. It makes sense as a long-term investment. The key word is *long-term*. Real estate is not a game of craps where you walk up, roll the dice a few times, and walk away with a wad of cash. A small minority of people have done that, but don't count on it.

You have two choices. You can pay for a landlord's mortgage to make him secure and equity-rich, or you can pay for your own mortgage to make yourself secure and equity-rich. So I say, anytime you can answer yes to the seven previous questions, it's a good time to buy a home.

👎 Bad Practice

Sitting on the sidelines, watching other people get ahead in real estate assets while you pay non-tax-deductible rent.

👍 Good Practice

Enjoying the pride and satisfaction of home ownership and taking advantage of the tax benefits home ownership brings.

Coming Up Next

A handy checklist that guides you from start to finish is next. This is a good tool for both home purchasing and home refinancing.

10

The Loan Process in Ten Easy Steps

I've seen loan process flowcharts that are so elaborate, with arrows going this way and that, I have to wonder if the author's purpose was to try to impress me with the complexity and enormity of their job. By contrast, here is a simple checklist that leads you through the steps, from start to finish. If you're a seasoned home-buyer, feel free to skip ahead to the next chapter.

Carolyn's Ten-Step Loan Process Checklist

✓**1.** Get a Good Faith Estimate and choose your loan officer.

A Good Faith Estimate (GFE) is a form that shows you your loan amount, interest rate, monthly payment, fees and costs, and other pertinent information. You can't logically choose a loan officer without first seeing the GFE, even if the loan officer is your best friend or brother. Ahead in Chapter 13, "How to Shop for a Loan Without Getting Tricked," I explain the GFE in detail, and you'll see why it is your first step in the loan process. Never fork over money to make an application—that is a scheme to reel you in, to commit you with your cash—and how could you reasonably make a commitment to giving your business to a particular lender or loan officer without *first* reviewing the cost of financing in the GFE?

When: Ask for a GFE and choose your loan officer when you're ready to go house hunting *and make an offer*. If you're just touring open houses to take mental notes for later, it's too early. If you plan to buy a house three months or more into the future, it's too early. You want the GFE to be fairly current and accurate. It shouldn't take more than two to three days to select a good loan officer and proceed to getting preapproved.

✓**2.** Get preapproved for solid financing.

A preapproval is a commitment from a lender for financing for a specific loan amount. To get preapproved, you must have a credit check, and most often, provide income and asset documentation as well. A preapproval can take from one to four days, depending on how busy they are. If you are ready to go house shopping, it is important to get preapproved first. Why? Because when you make an offer on a home, your real estate agent will need to present a copy of your preapproval letter along with your proposed purchase and sale agreement. (Some lenders call the pre-approval letter a commitment letter.) This lets the sellers know you have financing in place, and it gives you the power to negotiate. Without a preapproval letter, you will not be able to compete against other people making offers who have one. Naturally, you want a preapproval for your own security and peace of mind as well.

When: Don't make the colossal mistake of getting out on a limb with a signed purchase and sale agreement without having solid financial backing to close the deal. Get your preapproval right up front, and then you're secure and don't waste anyone's time.

✓**3.** Make an offer on a house, with the assistance of your buyer's agent.

Now for the fun: going house shopping. You can browse the Internet from your easy chair, but when it's time for the actual home tour, make sure you go with your buyer's agent. In Chapter 20, "Why You Need Agent Representation," I explain why having a real estate agent to represent you is as essential as having a preapproval letter from your loan officer. It's a free service to you that can save you from making one of many costly mistakes and prevent you from being ripped off.

When: Don't even think about presenting an offer without having a preapproval letter to accompany it. No home seller is going to take his or her property off the market without seeing that you have a real offer with financial backing. There have been far too many horror stories about purchase and sale agreements that became invalid when the potential homebuyer's loan was denied.

✓**4a.** Finalize the purchase and sale agreement and send a copy to your loan officer.

Once the price and other details have been negotiated, and both buyer and seller have signed the purchase and sale agreement, ask your buyer's agent to forward a copy to your loan officer. In addition, call your loan officer immediately with the good news that you have mutual acceptance.

When: It can take from several days to several weeks for a proposed purchase and sale agreement to be finalized and signed by all parties. If you're buying a bank-owned property, it takes longer because you're dealing with a committee or bank negotiator who is busy with other matters. Sometimes banks will wait to see if a higher offer comes in.

✓**4b.** Lock in your interest rate.

This is a big topic, so I've devoted Chapter 18, "When to Lock in Your Rate, When to Float," to the details, but I wanted to make you aware of it as you're going through the checklist.

When: Any time after you have a property address, you can lock in your rate to secure it from going up while your loan is in process.

✓**5.** Get a home inspection.

This step is actually outside the loan process, but it is not to be missed, so I'm listing it here anyway. Hire an independent, licensed home inspector and attend the inspection yourself, if at all possible. That way, the inspector can point out and show you any repairs that need to be done, such as dry rot or electrical or plumbing problems. You will receive a detailed report, which will be your basis for further negotiations, conducted by your real estate agent. If you have an FHA loan, a pest inspection is also required.

When: After you have a mutually accepted purchase and sale agreement, order the inspection right away. You need to determine that the property is in acceptable condition and negotiate with the seller (through your agent) any repair work you want taken care of before you take possession. Don't spend money on the appraisal report until this step is complete, just in case the inspection reveals something so major you decide against buying the property.

✓**6.** Simultaneously, work with your loan officer to provide all the documentation required.

Typically, your loan officer will need some information from you that you haven't provided yet, and now is the time to do so. For example:

• Pay stubs for one month pay, dated within 30 days of closing

• W2s, for the past two years

• If self-employed, two years' tax returns, all schedules, all pages

• Bank statement, dated within 30 days of closing, all pages

• If requested, a letter of explanation about employment or credit

• Name and phone number of your insurance agent for home-owner's insurance

• Copy of photo ID or signed Patriot Act form

• If a condo, contact information for the Homeowners' Association

When: When your loan officer asks for paperwork, hop on it right away. If there's a problem, let your loan officer know immediately, so he or she can help to find a solution. You'd be surprised at what solutions an experienced loan officer has in his or her arsenal. Never try to hide a fact, such as a tax lien, or an old judgment no one has mentioned in years; because I assure you, it will come out, and the sooner you deal with it, the better.

✓7. Your loan officer oversees ordering the appraisal and title report.

At this point, most lenders will need you to pay for the appraisal report. If your loan amount is above the conforming loan limit or a Jumbo Loan, two appraisals might be required. Typically, lenders will ask for credit card authorization so they can charge your credit card if the appraisal has been completed but the deal falls through. By law, you receive a copy of your appraisal report.

In the unusual event that there is a problem with the title, your loan officer will contact you; otherwise, you can assume all is well.

When: After you know for sure that your financing is in place and you are satisfied with the property inspection, the appraisal can be ordered by your lender. You do not order the appraisal yourself because lenders cannot accept appraisal reports ordered by consumers.

✓**8.** The underwriter conducts a final review and approval of your loan.

Once your loan file is complete, including title and appraisal, it goes to the underwriter for a final review. It's not unusual for the underwriter to ask for an additional piece of documentation; so if that happens, don't get upset. Provide it quickly, so your loan doesn't get held up. After your complete file has been approved, including the appraisal report, your loan goes to the doc draw department, and the loan documents are e-mailed to your closing agent (escrow agent or attorney, depending on your state).

When: The final review and approval may take 48 hours; or, in a busy time, it could take three weeks.

✓**9.** Sign your loan documents.

Your closing agent prints out your loan documents, and using the instructions provided by the lender, prepares the HUD-1 Settlement Statement, which shows the breakdown of your loan costs. You might say this is the final draft of the Good Faith Estimate you got at the beginning of the process. Then, he or she will call to set your appointment and to let you know how much money to bring in, in the form of a cashier's check, for the down payment and closing costs. Take your Good Faith Estimate, Interest Rate Lock Confirmation form, and personal identification with you. That way, if there's a mistake or, God forbid, a new bogus fee or bait and switch, you have your protection. Any errors can be corrected while you wait, so never sign a contract that is incorrect. If you cannot go into the agent's office, a mobile notary public may come out to you to sign the papers for a nominal fee. You receive a copy of all documents signed.

By the way, people do make mistakes from time to time. If you see something amiss on your loan documents, assume the best. Everyone is happy to apologize and correct a mishap while you wait. But if you do encounter an ugly surprise at the closing table and can't get it easily changed with the loan officer, still don't sign. Call the lender and ask to speak with the president or CEO. Tell him what the problem is and say, "I'd like your help in getting this error corrected because I don't want to be a victim of illegal bait and switch and have to file a complaint with the Attorney General." That should do it!

When: Your loan officer will direct you about your signing date. Please see the following step.

✓**10.** Your loan funds and you get the keys.

In some states, the loan closes when you sign the documents. That is called "table funding" because it's funded at the signing table. But in other states, your loan process is not finished yet. The documents are sent overnight back to the lender for review, a recording number is received from your local recorder's office, and then the escrow agent is authorized to close the loan. Why is there an escrow agent or attorney involved with the closing? Because federal law requires that a neutral middle party handle the disbursement of funds.

When: After your loan is closed, your real estate agent will provide you with the keys.

Cheers! Time to celebrate and move into your new home.

Coming Up Next

Where do you go to get your best loan? Do you apply online, over the phone, or swing on down to your local bank? What's the difference between a banker and a broker, and which is best?

11

Choose the Right Loan for YOU

This important chapter helps you with the basics: how to choose the right loan for your situation.

How Much Down Payment Is Required?

With the down payment, you are paying money up front toward your purchase to make your loan less than the purchase price. The down payment is the collateral for the lender; the larger your down payment, the less likely you are to walk away without paying, and that creates security for the lender.

- VA loan for U.S. Veterans: 0 down.
- FHA loan for your primary residence: 3.5 percent (of the purchase price) down.
- Conventional loan for your primary residence: probably 10 percent down.
  (If the county is considered to be in an area of declining values, you need 10 percent down. Otherwise, 5 percent down.)
- Conventional loan for an investment property: 20 percent down.
- Second home or vacation home: 20 percent down, because mortgage insurance companies will not insure these types of properties now.

Which Loan Program Is Best for You?

Here is a handy list of loan programs sorted out by what your situation might be. Read the subheads, and when you see the one that applies to you, look at the loan program recommended. Remember, these are my suggestions; the final choice is up to you.

Take a 30-Year Fixed Rate If...

- You plan to keep the property for a long time, at least five years.
- You want maximum security.
- The interest rate is low, at, or near the bottom.
- You might turn it into a rental property later.
- You are on a limited fixed income.

With a 30-year fixed rate, you won't have to worry about your rate or principal and interest payment changing. You can enjoy your low interest rate for the life of your loan, and you won't face the costs of refinancing later.

When the 30-year fixed rate mortgage is as low as an adjustable rate mortgage (or close to it), choose the fixed rate. When rates are low, choose the fixed rate so you'll be safe when they go up.

👎 Bad Practice

Teaser rate loans that are good only for the first two to three years.

👍 Good Practice

Long-term stability and security, which is what you get with the 30-year fixed rate and the 15-year fixed rate.

Take a 15-Year Fixed Rate If...

- You see retirement in your near future and want to be debt-free.
- Your income is excellent and you want to save money on interest.

When it comes to borrowing money, your number-one enemy is time. Most people think the number-one enemy is interest rate, but that's not so. Time is the greater factor in calculating the amount of your total payments. You can have a higher interest rate with a shorter term, and you end up paying less overall. For this reason, my personal choice is the 15-year fixed rate loan.

On your Truth-in-Lending form, you can see the total amount you will pay for your home. Let's look at two scenarios. Let's say you are buying a home for $200,000 and the interest rate is 6 percent interest. You want to compare a 15-year loan with a 30-year loan—the following box shows the calculations.

$200,000 at 6% Interest

Total payments with the 30-year loan = $431,677.

Total payments with the 15-year loan = $303,788.

You save $127,889 with the 15-year loan.

In reality, you would save even more because you get a lower interest rate on a 15-year loan.

Of course, you can take the 30-year loan but pay it off in 15 years. Some people prefer this option because you aren't obligated to the higher payment on months when you might have additional expenses. This is a good point. However, if you are comfortable with the 15-year loan payment, I like the lower interest rate—and then you can pay that off even faster, saving even more money.

Take an Interest Only (IO) Loan If...

- You want to get your start in real estate now and are having a challenge qualifying with your current income, which is increasing.
- You are young and your income is still rising rapidly.
- You are buying in an area where values are increasing and you need a lower payment.

The IO Loan is never my first choice, but there is a time and place for this program. You pay the interest portion of the payment only, so you have a lower payment, which is important if your debt-to-income ratio is tight. The downside is that you are not paying down the balance, so it's kind of like renting from yourself. Keep in mind that the interest-only payment will last for a limited time, and when the payment increases to include both the principal and interest—on a shorter timeline now—your payment will increase significantly. To explain further...

If the interest-only period is for 10 years, when the payment adjusts to include both principal and interest, it is going to be calculated for the 20 years remaining. So your payment increases in two ways: (1) by including the principal buy-down, and (2) by cramming it into the 20 years remaining, as opposed to amortizing it over 30 years, like the traditional 30-year fixed rate. If your income has increased, handling the larger payment might be no problem, and this loan would have served its purpose in getting you into owning real estate sooner than you could have otherwise.

👎 Bad Practice

Taking an Interest Only Loan to squeeze into a house you cannot really afford and will not be able to afford when the IO period ends. That is a plan for financial disaster.

> 👍 **Good Practice**
>
> Carefully considering an Interest Only Loan when your circum-
> stance meets *all* of the make-sense criteria: Your income is increas-
> ing, the value is increasing, and you aren't using the IO payment as
> an excuse to overbuy.

Most IO Loans have a fixed-rate period for either the first five or
ten years.

When the IO period ends, you might want to sell or refinance. If
the value of your property has increased, that shouldn't be a problem,
but as soon as you can afford to pay toward the principal balance, I
highly recommend doing so. The sooner you can decrease the
amount of money you owe, the better. When you pay off a loan that is
6.5 percent interest, it's like you are investing at 6.5 percent in interest. Not bad!

Take a High Balance Loan If...

- You need a loan over $417,000 and you live in a high-cost area.

The High Balance Loan is a program for people living in high-
cost areas where the median home price is higher than the average in
the United States. With this program, you can get a 30-year fixed rate
cheaper than with the Jumbo Loan program (and for many Jumbo
Loan amounts, no fixed rate is available). The loan size depends on
the county. The maximum for 2009 on a one-unit property in the con-
tinental United States is $729,750. To check on what it is for your
county, ask your loan officer or go online at http://www.fhfa.gov/Get-
File.aspx?FileID=134.

The cost for a High Balance Loan is higher than for a conforming
loan, and you have a choice of paying that with a higher up-front fee
or a higher rate (or a little of both). Your loan officer can quote you
current pricing.

Take the 5/1 ARM or 7/1 ARM If...

- You need a Jumbo Loan.

The 5/1 ARM (adjustable rate mortgage) and 7/1 ARM will save you money on loan amounts that are too high for the conventional loan (and possibly the High Balance Conforming Loan).

If your loan is higher than the conventional limit, your loan is considered to be a Jumbo Loan. These loans are riskier for the investor because of the amount of money involved, so they have a higher interest rate to offset the risk.

When the conventional 30-year fixed rate is 6 percent, the jumbo 30-year fixed rate might be 7.375 percent. The box below shows what a difference that can make to your payment.

$600,000 on a 6% Conventional Loan and a 7.375% Jumbo Loan

$600,000 @ 6% = $3,597 principal and interest payment

$600,000 @ 7.375% = $4,144 principal and interest payment

A difference of $547/mo. and $6,564/year.

Over five years, the difference is $32,823 in interest.

So how do you avoid shoveling out an extra $32,000 in interest payments? By taking a 5/1 or 7/1 ARM. It makes good sense.

The loan is fixed for the first five or seven years. Then, it will adjust yearly thereafter. Typically, these loans have either no prepayment penalty or only a one-year prepayment penalty, so you're free to refinance early if you want. Make sure you know whether your loan will have a prepayment penalty. If you don't plan to flip it in less than 12 months, there's no harm in having a one-year prepay penalty, and you might get a loan with zero points (no Origination Fee) as a result.

You'll get a lower interest rate with the 5/1 ARM than with the 7/1 ARM. Check with your loan officer because the amount of variance changes, making it impossible for me to quote rate differences here.

Take an Option ARM Only If...

- You are financially independent and choose this for cash flow or investment reasons.

The Option ARM is a valid tool for the man or woman who could pay cash but chooses to invest their money elsewhere for financial advantage.

👎 Bad Practice

Taking a pick-a-payment Option ARM loan because you need the minimum, temporary payment.

👍 Good Practice

Taking an Option ARM if you are a savvy investor, fully understand the loan, and know how to use your extra cash to increase your wealth.

The megaproblem that occurred during the mortgage meltdown of 2007–2008 is that a lot of folks on modest incomes were seduced into taking the Option ARM. They were blinded by the so-called fantastic rate of 1 percent or 2 percent. In their haste to grab the deal, they didn't stop to figure out that rates weren't really that low, and it was too good to be true. And the greedy loan sharks who sold those loans were so caught up in making $40,000 and $50,000 off of the one loan, they buried their consciences. Some of those loan offers had no more than a high school education, and they were making close to a half-million dollars a year. That's a lot of temptation.

World Savings was known for promoting the Option ARM. The account executives traveled around to mortgage broker offices giving slick presentations, saying that everyone should take advantage of this loan. Then, Washington Mutual Bank rolled out their Option ARM, as did dozens of other companies. They sold these loans like popcorn at the movies, but not long later, they turned to poison, and the foreclosures poured in. When the 2 percent honeymoon ended and the payments rose sharply, the homeowners discovered two things: (1) They could no longer afford to make their house payment. (2) And, they had no equity left because their balance actually went up every month. That was a feature many of them never understood. As a result, lots of those good folks are now renters with trashed credit.

👎 Bad Practice

Refinancing into an Option ARM because you overspent on your credit cards, and someone is encouraging you to use your home equity as your piggy bank.

👍 Good Practice

Preserving your precious home equity; and if it makes sense to refinance, taking a secure fixed interest rate.

When interest rates are 6 percent and the bank lets you pay only 2 percent, the extra 4 percent is added to your loan balance for you to pay later. Your balance goes up each and every month—not down like a normal loan. This is called negative amortization. I can't tell you how many angry people I've spoken with who never understood that. They were shocked to discover they owed more than they started off with and now it was impossible for them to refinance.

It made me heartsick when I heard disc jockeys on a Christian radio station recommend this loan to all their listeners. They knew gospel music, but they didn't know mortgages, and they were telling their trusting audience to call a certain mortgage company I knew to be liars. I was so upset, I had to turn off the radio.

(I proved them to be liars when I conducted my Mortgage Mystery Shopping Experiment and collected Good Faith Estimates from ten mortgage lenders, which is explained in my first book, *Mortgage Rip-Offs and Money Savers*.)

Nevertheless, there is a valid place and time for the Option ARM. When it was first rolled out, its nickname was "The Wealthy Man's Loan."

Later, when companies tried to sugarcoat the negative amortization feature and mass market it, they nicknamed it "The Pick-a-Payment Loan." That's because each month you can choose to make the minimum payment, a partial payment, or the full payment.

So, back to the wealthy borrower. For the person who knows how to use a negative amortization loan to their advantage, it's a valid option. You accept a 6 percent rate, pay just 2 percent, invest the bulk of your money at 12 percent; and then in a few years, pull out your investment and pay off the mortgage.

Oh yes, and in case you're wondering how those greedy loan sharks made a fortune selling Option ARMs, it is because they jacked up the margins and tacked on prepayment penalties. Of course, they never mentioned those things if the borrowers didn't ask—and most of them never thought to do so. That's because they weren't savvy investors and had no business taking out that type of loan in the first place.

12 Questions to Ask Before You Take an Option ARM

1. How long does the initial rate last?
2. How often will the rate adjust?
3. What is the index and how stable is it?
4. What is the margin?
5. What is the Yield Spread Premium?
6. What is the margin at par rate?
7. What is the minimum payment cap?
8. What is the negative amortization cap?
9. What is the lifetime interest rate cap?
10. What can my payment go to, on a worse-case scenario basis?
11. What is the payment recast (recalculation) period?
12. Does the loan have a conversion option, and what is the conversion fee?

Coming Up Next

Where is the best place to go for your home loan? My answer, coming up next, just might surprise you. And get a load of the rip-off artist who posed as a helpful loan officer. Watch out for people like that!

12

Broker, Banker, or Direct Lender?

Where is the best place to get your loan? Bank, mortgage broker, or direct lender?

Read this true story for the inside scoop. Kay worked first for a national direct lending company, and that's where I met her, sitting at a large oak desk taking loan applications by phone. She was the queen of loan applications.

I asked, "How do you get more apps than anyone else here?"

Beaming, she said, "I tell them whatever they want to hear."

Kay was recently hired and didn't fully understand the business. All she knew was that she was supposed to take three applications a day, so to accomplish that, she agreed to whatever the person on the other end of the phone said they wanted. As you can imagine, a lot of those in-coming loans turned into disasters. So she moved on.

Next, she worked for a mortgage broker. Shortly, Kay was caught in an ugly bait-and-switch snafu. She gave the homebuyers a Good Faith Estimate with a low interest rate, and then when they went to their loan signing, they were shocked to see the rate was 2 percent higher. That makes a huge difference in monthly payment, but they felt stuck and signed anyway. They were so infuriated, they filed a complaint with the Attorney General's office, who in turn, issued a big fine to the brokerage she worked for. So once again, she moved on.

After that, she got hired by a good national bank you'd all recognize. Her sweet-talking skills were excellent, so I'm sure the managers were snowed at the interview. I don't know what kind of mess she made there, but I did find out that when she moved on again, she stole the bank's five-thousand-dollar laptop computer.

I'm sure you wouldn't want to do business with Miss Kay, would you?

Notice that she was at a direct lender, a mortgage broker, and a bank. No matter which type of institution you went to, you could have found yourself filling out a loan application with Kay—or someone like her.

Find Your Mortgage Star

Now then, you've probably already figured out my answer to the question, where is the best place to get a mortgage? You don't pick by institution. There are incompetent employees everywhere. There are also honest, expert loan officers in all types of lending institutions. They are the good, hard-working, transparent, ethical mortgage people who sleep at night with a good conscience because they treat all their clients right.

So the answer is that you choose the individual you want to work with, not by the institution.

Price should not be your only consideration. Working with a loan officer who has the experience and expertise to handle a potentially fatal problem that pops up can make the difference in your loan going through or going bust. And you never know what surprise might come hurtling at you like a sudden tsunami. Here's an example. Recently, I had a wonderful client, a nice young couple who are buying their first home. They want to get out of noisy New York, and they find their dream home at an affordable price in the Poconos. Everything goes smoothly, and we are at the final stage before printing the loan documents for signing, the final review by the underwriter. Suddenly, we get hit with a surprise.

Their loan is "suspended." The underwriter refuses to approve it because the commute from their new home to their workplace is 110 miles. She says the mortgage insurance company will not insure the loan under that circumstance, and that they will have to put 20 percent down instead of 10 percent if they want to buy this home.

But they don't have the funds to put 20 percent down. I ask if there is a rep. from the MI company I can talk to about getting an exception, because the couple hopes to transfer to offices that are closer to their new home in the near future. The answer is no. No rep. to talk to and absolutely no exceptions to the rule.

How am I going to call and tell these excited homebuyers their loan just died—now, when they are at the end of the process? I am told, "Too bad, but it's out of our control. There's nothing we can do about the mortgage insurance companies' guidelines." It is a terrible sinking-into-a-dark-hole kind of feeling.

But wait.

I don't operate that way. I am a homebuyer's advocate, and I don't accept a denial that easily. So I go on the Internet and locate a central phone number for the mortgage insurance company. I call and ask to speak with an underwriter who handles Pennsylvania properties. I explain the story and dilemma and ask under what circumstances they would approve a commute of 110 miles.

"Don't say they hope to transfer to a closer office in the future; that's not what we want to hear," she tells me. That's enlightening. Then I ask her what it is she does want to hear. In other words, I ask for the answers in her answer book. She coaches me on what to write in a letter of explanation about the commute. I thank her and ask for her permission to use her name in my letter, and she is happy to oblige.

I write a fantastic letter with four bullet points and respectfully submit it to our underwriter, asking for the suspension to be over-turned. Twenty minutes later, I get back the underwriter's response: loan approved.

That's what I'm talking about when I say there is a big the advantage of having an expert loan officer represent you. A true mortgage star handles the drama while you sit home relaxed. A novice or mediocre loan officer accepts the denial and breaks your heart. (If you have a long commute and need a copy of my letter, send me an email via www.AskCarolynWarren.com.)

> **👎 Bad Practice**
>
> Calling a particular bank or lender "good" or "bad." Two loan officers working at the same lender might price their loans and handle challenges differently.

> **👍 Good Practice**
>
> Collecting five business cards from your favorite loan officer—one to keep and four to give out to friends. Choose by individual, not by institution.

What About Credit Unions?

I've worked for a direct lender, a mortgage broker, and a bank (as well as a wholesale account executive and mobile notary signer), but I have never worked for a credit union. I used to say, "I've never met a credit union I couldn't beat," and it was true. As a broker, I could beat their rate by .25 percent every time—until some good folks who used my consulting service sent me Good Faith Estimates from their local credit unions.

I found that when the credit union was directly connected with an employer, they could have some incredible rates. For example, one gentleman who worked for NASA showed me the GFE from the NASA credit union, and it was amazing. But give me a GFE from a credit union serving the general public, and I'll go to a wholesale lender and beat it 99 percent of the time.

Therefore, I stand by my advice of choosing by individual loan officer rather than by the institution. I can tell you from personal experience that two loan officers at the same institution will price the identical loan very differently. One loan officer might say, "I've got three loans this month, so these three need to pay my bills." Whereas another loan officer will say, "I give everybody the cheapest pricing I can and I build my volume that way."

Same office—different philosophies of doing business. I know loan officers who price their loans so high, they need only one loan per month to make a living; and yet, just down the hall, there are other loan officers who do the cheapest loans ever.

Coming Up Next

How to find your mortgage star and how to shop for a loan—all tips from someone who's been behind closed doors in the mortgage industry, next.

13

How to Shop for a Loan Without Getting Tricked

Bad loans that look good on the surface, hidden junk fees, big back-end commissions you pay for, bait-and-switch tactics—with all the pitfalls out there, how do you shop for a loan?

Some of the worst advice I've ever read comes from "how-to" articles printed online and in newspapers. The writers have never worked in the mortgage industry, and they think they're offering helpful tips, when in fact, they're steering you all wrong. Here's what I'm talking about...

Bad Advice Disguised as a Helpful Tip

I found the following advice both online and in newspapers. When I showed it to other loan officers, they rolled their eyes, grunted in disgust, or went off on a rant about how stupid it was. The point is, all mortgage loan officers were unanimous in their agreement that these so-called tips steer you wrong.

"Shop Deep and Wide"

What a waste of time and energy! Not only that, but it's likely to lead you away from a good, ethical loan officer and right into the clutches of a smooth-talking loan shark.

Loan officers peg people who are shopping a long list of companies as "rate shoppers"—people who are a waste of their time. The honest loan officers who quote you the actual rate of the day know they're competing against liars who underquote just to get you in the door; and they know that if they don't choose to join their game of deception, they don't stand a chance of getting the rate shoppers' business. Invariably, the rate shoppers will go with the underquote rather than with their honest quote; therefore, why should they spend their time working up a Good Faith Estimate?

I saw a coffee mug on a loan officer's desk that read, "What do I look like, an Information Booth?" It's funny because it strikes a nerve. Loan officers tire of being used for information by people who have no intention of doing business with them. These are what I call time shoplifters, and they abuse the professional who depends on commissions to make a living. When these information gatherers take up half an hour of a loan officer's time, they have just caused the loan officer to work for zero pay. I'm sure you can see how loan officers have a problem when a dozen of these information gatherers attack them every day.

And here's a glimpse behind the scenes: Managers conduct meetings for their loan officers on how to handle rate shoppers. I've sat in meetings where they tell their loan officers to quote a quarter-point low. "Everyone else is doing it," is the justification. They consider it mandatory for their survival. And on forums for mortgage professionals, the topic comes up. Some explain how to divert the rate shopper's attention away from interest rate and slide into taking the application.

You might think that's sneaky and unfair, and maybe it is. But I'm telling you that calling a long list asking for the rate of the day is a good way to get tricked and a bad way to go about the loan process.

Just this week, I received an email from a homebuyer who asked just one question: "What are your lender fees?" Her email might as well have said, "I'm clueless about getting a mortgage." Any loan officer could say they have zero lender fees, because lender fees can be disguised as a discount fee instead or paid by the Yield Spread Premium. So that question alone is just as meaningless as asking, "What's your rate?"

"Ask Ten Questions"

More dreadful advice! I can just picture you sitting at your kitchen table with a big pad of paper and the telephone. You call the first lender in the phone book and proceed to pepper him or her with ten questions. Twenty-eight minutes later, you've got three pages of notes, which include a list of the lender fees. Then, you call the second lender and do the same. More pages of notes, but this time you get a whole new perspective as this lender has no lender fees but the interest rate is higher. This is getting interesting, you think, and eagerly dial the third lender. The loan officer asks what quotes you've gotten so far, and after you explain the one with lender fees and a lower rate and the other with no lender fees and the higher rate, this loan officer tells you about Yield Spread Premium (the cash rebate paid to a mortgage broker based on an interest rate above the wholesale par rate), and you jot down three more pages of notes. Wow, what an education you're getting! You dial the fourth lender, and this time you know to ask about Yield Spread Premium. But the loan officer tells you they don't have that because they're a bank, and goes on to say you should avoid paying a "middleman fee" and go with a bank. That seems reasonable, but when the bank's interest rate is just as high, it doesn't add up. Plus, the mortgage broker told you banks are retail, and they are wholesale. It's getting confusing now, but you forge ahead and dial the fifth lender. This loan officer sounds really sweet and friendly, and she tells you she has the lowest rate and no points. No points sounds appealing, but then you discover she has six different lender fees that add up to more than the one point you were quoted before, so you smell something fishy. Two days, ten phone calls, and 30 pages of scribbles later, you're more confused than when you started. You're wasting a lot of time, just like Leanne in Chapter 1, "Getting the World's Cheapest Loan." You have to wonder if there isn't a better way to figure out which lender has the best loan.

There is.

Instead of shopping till you drop, first select your loan officer. Then *after* you have chosen your honest advocate, your mortgage star, you can ask all the questions you want. You'll feel good about this for two reasons: (1) You can be confident the answers you receive are true and accurate. (2) You can have a good conscience, knowing you are not shoplifting someone's time.

Here's a tip from inside the business: Once a loan officer knows you are employing their services, they are most happy to answer each and every question you have; and they will look out for your best interests by recommending cost-saving options. Good loan officers build their reputations on providing you with financial education, getting you a good deal, and facilitating a smooth transaction. So once you've made your commitment, you don't need to worry or expend energy watching your back.

Now that we've established that your first step is to select the right loan officer, exactly how do you go about doing that?

👎 Bad Practice

Going through an exhausting search for a loan by quizzing ten loan officers.

👍 Good Practice

Choose your loan officer first, and then ask your questions. This is time efficient for you, and you can feel secure in the answers you receive.

How to Find a Mortgage Star

I like to call the hard-working mortgage professionals who act as your advocate, getting you the best loan at the cheapest price that they can—with full disclosure and clear communication—mortgage stars. That's who you want to work with.

Follow my method, and you'll never have to worry about being taken advantage of. Locate your personal mortgage star by skipping the lengthy phone conversation and asking for a Good Faith Estimate. It takes less than two minutes to say, "My name is Carolyn Warren, and I am in the market to buy a house. I'm looking in the

$250,000 price range, and I have ten percent to put down. My credit score is 805. Will you please e-mail me a Good Faith Estimate so I can see what my loan would look like?"

👎 Bad Practice

Asking, "What's your interest rate today?" as a means of finding a good loan officer. Verbal quotes are meaningless.

👍 Good Practice

Asking for a Good Faith Estimate as a means of finding a good loan officer. If you like the pricing, then ask about experience and their ability to handle unexpected challenges.

The loan officer might have a couple of questions such as property taxes, whether you're a W2 employee or self-employed, and who might be on the loan with you. But no credit check needs to be done if you already know your credit score, so you should not give out your Social Security number at this point.

If the loan officer insists on having all your personal information to complete an application and pull your credit before providing you with the GFE, then that is a loan officer you don't need to work with. (Remember Leanne's story in Chapter 1?) You want to avoid having your credit pulled multiple times before you've chosen your loan officer because it is possible that it could negatively impact your score. This is a concern if your score is borderline to 740, 720, 700, 620, or 600. Those are the lines of demarcation for a higher interest rate right now; check with your loan officer because credit requirements change.

Some loan officers will tell you, "A Good Faith Estimate isn't worth the paper it's written on."

And to them I say, "Speak for yourself. My GFEs are a valuable tool and very informative, as are the GFEs written by scores of other honest loan officers."

What's more, you can always ask for a written guarantee that the lender fees will not vary by more than ten percent, as protection that the GFE is not worthless. I provide my clients with a nice guarantee in a separate document, but an e-mail saying the same is sufficient. Print it out and keep it with your GFE as protection against bait and switch.

Then go one step further and ask about their experience and ability to handle challenges, should something unexpected come up. Listen carefully as sometimes what they don't say is just as revealing as what they do say. Listen to your gut instinct. How confident do you feel with this person?

How to Handle a "Forgotten" Fee

Good folks from across the country have e-mailed me saying their loan officer "forgot" to include a $500-plus fee that showed up on the Settlement Statement at the loan signing. Ha! I don't believe it—the loan officer was afraid you'd object to their big bogus fee, so he "accidentally-on-purpose" left it off until you got to the signing. He knows people won't object when they've got their household goods all boxed up ready to move. If this happens to you, prove him wrong!

If someone tries to slip in extra charges that weren't disclosed, pull out your GFE and guarantee, and then sweetly say, "I see there is an error here. That $500 charge was not on my Good Faith Estimate. Let's call the lender and have that corrected because I won't sign the Settlement Statement or Truth-in-Lending form until it's been taken care of. Would you like to do it while I wait, or should we reschedule?"

👎 Bad Practice

Signing loan papers you disagree with just because you're on a deadline for closing and moving. Refuse to be victimized.

👍 Good Practice

Comparing the Settlement Statement with the Good Faith Estimate. Have errors corrected while you wait before you put your signature on the line.

Because your escrow agent or attorney can call the lender and have it fixed on the spot, you'll probably wait. It takes about 15 minutes to redo the necessary forms and e-mail them. In the meantime, you can go ahead and sign the rest of the paperwork.

Stand your ground and refuse to be bullied into signing documents that are not correct. Believe me, no loan officer in the world is going to let your loan fall out over $500. Loan officers work on a commission basis, and if the deal doesn't close, they have spent weeks working for zero income. So even if the fee was genuinely forgotten, they need to stand by their Good Faith Estimate and "eat" the cost. Good loan officers will do that. If they forget to tell you about the processing fee, then they pay for it out of their own commissions. That's the way it works—if you refuse to be a victim. So you see, the GFE is valuable and something you keep and take to your signing.

If loan officers try to persuade you to skip the GFE because it's "worthless," you can thank them for letting you know *their* GFEs are no good and then promptly move on to someone else. Obviously, that person is not a mortgage star. Don't let one of those shysters coerce you into jumping over the GFE straight into pulling your credit report for a preapproval.

Why You Need the Good Faith Estimate Before Making a Decision

The Good Faith Estimate is a summary of your loan terms. It spells out important information, such as the following:

- Loan type
- Loan amount
- Interest rate
- Lender fees
- Third-party loan costs
- Unnecessary junk fees (disguised with legitimate sounding names)
- Property taxes to be paid up front

- Homeowner's insurance to be paid up front
- Prepaid interest for the days between closing and the end of the month
- How much cash you'll need to close, including down payment and closing costs
- Your projected monthly payment
- Monthly mortgage insurance fee, if applicable

Now that is a lot of vital information! Never, ever proceed with your loan or shell out money for the appraisal report before you have reviewed your Good Faith Estimate.

Federal law requires lenders to provide you with a GFE within three business days of making an application, but there is no reason why a loan officer cannot give you one right from the start. I think it's absurd for a homebuyer to make a commitment to do business with a lender without first seeing what the cost is. Would you commit to buying an automobile without first seeing what your interest rate and monthly payment will be? No, of course not. Then why would you proceed with a mortgage without first receiving all the vital information on the GFE?

This is the time to sort the wheat from the chaff. If you see nonsense like "Other Fees," "Miscellaneous Fees," "Ancillary Fees," "Satisfaction Fees," or other ambiguous terms, then you know you're looking at chaff, the garbage.

This is also the time to look for the Yield Spread Premium. More about this in Chapter 15, "Five Things You Need to Know About YSP," but if the mortgage broker fails to state it in an estimated dollar amount, you've got someone who is afraid of full disclosure, not a mortgage star.

Those are two obvious things to look for, but what else do you need to be aware of when you're reviewing the GFE? Don't miss "Seven Ways They Can Trick You on the Good Faith Estimate" in Chapter 17, "The Good Faith Estimate: Tricks and Traps." But first...

Coming Up Next

When you read your Good Faith Estimate, you'll see a list of fees. Which ones are legitimate and which ones are bogus add-ons designed to boost the lender's profit at your expense? This is a hot topic that reaches right down to your wallet.

14

The Truth About Fees

What's up with all the loan fees? Are they all mandatory, or are some bogus junk fees that you can get waived? This chapter alone could easily save you 50 times the cost of this book, so I hope you'll keep it for future reference and recommend it to other homebuyers and homeowners who are refinancing. I am all for getting rid of excess costs. But, some people try so hard to get reduced fees that they end up shooting themselves in the pocketbook. They fuss over a couple hundred dollars and pay thousands more as a result. Take care you don't accidentally make that mistake. To illustrate, here's a true story:

Mr. and Mrs. Thrifty, as I call them, wanted so much to get the cheapest loan ever that they made two costly errors. (1) They refused to pay for mandatory fees, and (2) they lied about what they could afford. Here's what happened...

They asked for par rate, the lowest rate available without paying extra. The loan officer gave them par rate at 5.75 with a 1 percent Origination Fee. Par rate with 1 percentage point is fair and customary, but the Thriftys wanted something better, so Mrs. Thrifty called the loan officer and insisted that they needed the 1 percent loan Origination Fee to be reduced.

"We really can't bring in that much cash to closing because we don't have the money. We simply don't have the cash to pay for a 1 percent Origination Fee," she said.

"No problem," said the loan officer. "It is the company policy to make 1 percent on a loan, so I can reduce the Origination Fee to whatever you want and the rest can be made up in the Yield Spread

Premium (the back-end commission for taking a higher rate). Do you want a zero Origination Fee with a rate of 6 percent instead?"

"Oh no! We cannot pay 6 percent!" Mrs. Thrifty sounded horrified at the thought, like she might faint from shock. "We need the 5.75 rate, but we cannot pay more than .375 in an Origination Fee."

The conversation went on for awhile with the loan officer explaining you have a choice between a lower up-front fee or a lower interest rate, but Mrs. Thrifty insisted on having it both ways.

"Okay, no problem. I'll reduce your Origination Fee to .375," said the exasperated loan officer. Because there was no reasoning with Mrs. Thrifty, the loan officer agreed to the reduced fee. But they were going to have to take a higher rate because no lender is going to do a loan for only .375 total profit—as that isn't enough to stay in business. Because they were still waiting for the seller to accept their offer, the Thriftys weren't locking in their rate yet anyway. The loan officer decided to stop arguing and just wait to see what the rates were like when they were ready to lock in.

Mrs. Thrifty said, "Thank you. You know, we just need to have very, very low fees because we don't have much money for closing costs."

"I understand," said the loan officer.

About a week later, the signed purchase and sale agreement arrived. Mrs. Thrifty went back into super negotiation mode, this time about the other fees.

"I'm looking at the Good Faith Estimate, and the underwriting fee is too high. What can you do about it? We can't pay so much. Do you know what I'm saying? We have to have a lower underwriting fee. I really feel like it's too much to pay," she said.

"Yes, I understand. I'll see what can be done," said the loan officer. She didn't want to lose the loan over a couple hundred dollars, but the wholesale lenders don't negotiate their underwriting fee for anyone, not even their own grandmothers.

Mrs. Thrifty added, "And we don't like the processing fee either. I think that's a junk fee. Can you get rid of that fee, too?"

"The processing fee is not junk. We hire an independent loan processor who works many hours behind the scenes on your loan setting up the appraisal, title, escrow, getting the file in perfect shape for underwriting, and so on. That money goes to her, and believe me, she is worth every penny," said the loan officer.

"But we can't pay so much. We have very limited funds to bring in. We can't pay high fees. We can barely make the down payment with our savings. Can you see what you can do about the processing fee? This other company we checked with had a lower fee."

The loan officer saw that there was no reasoning with her client and she felt that Mrs. Thrifty was threatening to go to another company, so she said, "Sure, I'll check into it and get back to you."

When the loan officer called Mrs. Thrifty back, she said, "Good news. Your Origination Fee is .375 as you requested, and I got both the underwriting fee and processing fee cut in half for you."

Mrs. Thrifty said she was so happy and thanked her very much. She probably thought her whining and begging paid off. But wait, that's not the end of the story. Remember, the company policy was to make 1 percent on each loan? Policy is policy, and it's fair and customary. So by reducing the Origination Fee, the underwriting fee, and the processing fee, it was necessary to raise the interest rate so that the Origination Fee plus the Yield Spread Premium would equal 1 percent. This meant they could not get par rate, the lowest interest rate available without paying extra to buy down the rate.

A few days later, the Thriftys faxed in their updated bank statements. The loan officer saw that all the fussing about not having enough money to cover both the down payment and the closing costs was a whole lot of hot air. After making the down payment and paying the closing costs, the Thriftys had excess money in the amount of $60,000. There was no shortage of funds at all. Their whopping lie about not having the funds to pay for the customary fees annoyed the loan officer.

Meanwhile, interest rates had dropped. The par rate went down to 5.25 percent. But the Thriftys' rate was locked in at 5.875%.

Because they made a huge fuss over fees, they paid five-eighths higher, which made their monthly payment approximately $142 more per month on their $360,000 loan. They would have been better off paying the up-front cost, which they could easily afford, and getting a significantly lower rate, because after only 16 months, they would have come out ahead with the lower rate.

Why "No Fees" Can Cost You More

One popular marketing ploy is to advertise "No Fees!"

Don't be duped. Any company can give you no fees; they just raise the interest rate to make up for it.

Today, a homebuyer called me for a consultation about his loan offers. He had an excellent Good Faith Estimate from a mortgage broker, but his real estate agent told him to call a popular big bank we all know. The bank was advertising "no fees," and that sounded good.

I took a look at his GFEs for a loan of $200,000. Which would you choose?

Which Offer Is Better?

Mortgage Broker	Big Bank
5.875%	6.75%
$750 Lender Fee + Third-Party Costs	0 Fees
Payment: $1,183/mo.	$1,297/mo.

Would you pay $114 more each month to avoid fees? You would if you genuinely lacked money to cover the cost and didn't care about payment. But if you keep the home for more than a few years, you'll come out ahead by paying the fees and taking the lower interest rate.

Ideally, you want to cover the fair and customary costs yourself, but avoid the unnecessary, bogus fees that are tacked on just to pad profits. And believe me, I am 100 percent against those absurd fees; so let's talk about which is which next.

Do You Really Have to Pay That?

Some fees are necessary and some are bogus. Here, I offer my personal opinion, based on more than a dozen years working in both retail and wholesale lending.

Two Customary Lender Fees

The following are services required on all loans. They must be paid for in some way. Either (1) you pay for them up front, (2) you pay for them via a fee by a different name, or (3) you pay for them by taking a higher interest rate.

Underwriting or Administration

The underwriter reviews the entire loan file, including your application, your income and asset documents, the title report, the appraisal report, the purchase and sale agreement, and everything else in the file. The underwriter makes a determination on whether the paperwork is sufficient to support the investor's requirement to back the loan, and he or she issues the final approval.

Lenders charge an underwriting fee to help pay the salaries of the underwriters. Sometimes, they'll call it an administration fee instead. It doesn't matter—as long as you don't pay both underwriting and administration. I call that "double dipping" into your wallet, and that is unacceptable.

The fee varies, but wholesale lenders commonly charge $700–$995 now. A mortgage broker might choose to pass on all of that fee to you or cover part of it with his commission. If you see an underwriting fee of $250, you can bet it's being supplemented by the loan officer to be competitive. If you're in the Midwest, you'll see lower fees; and if you're in California or New York, expect higher fees.

Some people ask, "My loan is only $80,000. Why do I have to pay the same underwriting fee as a person whose loan is $400,000? It doesn't seem fair."

The answer is, "Because there's just as much paperwork and just as much time involved in reviewing and approving a small loan as a large one."

This week, I saw a Good Faith Estimate that had no underwriting or administration fee; but there was a $590 Funding Fee. What a hoot! So beware of lenders that call a standard fee by another name.

> 👎 **Bad Practice**
>
> Refusing to pay required loan costs when you can easily afford them. If you force your loan officer to cover them for you, you'll have to take a higher interest rate.

> 👍 **Good Practice**
>
> Paying your closing cost fees or having the seller pay your fees as part of your purchase and sale agreement.

Processing Fee

A good loan officer and a good processor make an awesome team. The loan officer brings in the business, takes the application, and oversees the loan from beginning to end. But the processor manages a myriad of details behind the scenes. Typically, the processor orders the title, the appraisal, the verification of employment, and the insurance binder. She sends disclosures to the borrowers, making sure the loan file is compliant with all federal regulations. After the initial approval, she works with the loan officer on loan conditions and unexpected problems that arise—as they invariably do—shielding the client customer from much stress. She sets up the closing with the escrow officer or attorney. She is a detail-oriented person who handles a barrage of phone calls and e-mail messages every day while simultaneously putting together the complete loan package. When everything has been completed, she submits the loan to the underwriter for final review and approval. She has relationships with the underwriters and funders, which comes in handy more often than you would like to think.

This fee varies by region and lender—up to $495 is not uncommon.

👎 Bad Practice

Making a commitment by paying an application fee before you've received a Good Faith Estimate outlining the costs of the loan.

👍 Good Practice

Getting a Good Faith Estimate up front, choosing your loan officer, and then proceeding with your detailed questions, loan processing, and paying any up-front costs that are required.

Two Optional Lender Fees

Lenders come up with creative ways to make their loans look cheaper than their competitors, or to combat time shoplifters. Take a look at these two fees.

Application Fee

Some lenders charge this as a temporary fee to combat customer abuse. It's sad, but they get so many people asking for quotes and GFEs and asking ten stupid questions before they even have a loan approved that take up their whole day and then these rude time shoplifters never get back to them, disappearing into the silent void without so much as a thank you, so the loan officers end up working hours and hours for free every week.

What you need to realize is that loan officers work on a commission-only basis. They get paid zero if they don't close a loan, so when you take their time gathering information, they are working for nothing, hoping to get your business. That's fine as long as you don't take up an excessive amount of time at this point. Once you've chosen your loan officer, you can ask that person as many questions as you want, and no question will be considered stupid or superfluous. The loan officer who is getting your business is happy to spend time help-ing you. It's just nonsensical to ask all kinds of detailed questions before you even know whether you're going to be working with that professional. Also I have to say, when you ask loan officers for a Good Faith Estimate, at least have the courtesy to get back to them and let them know what your decision is. It's discourteous to leave them hanging.

It takes valuable time out of the workday to prepare an accurate GFE, so don't ask a loan officer to send you three different ones unless you've made a commitment to work with that loan officer. You don't need a separate GFE for a 10-year loan, a 15-year loan, and a 30-year loan. The fees don't vary by loan term. To compare the monthly payments for the three different scenarios, go to www.Mort-gageHelper.com and use the handy calculator. There is no login required, and you can play with numbers to your heart's content.

If a loan officer receives too many requests for free GFEs each and every day, he or she hardly has time to get any actual income-pro-ducing work done.

To combat this problem, some companies used to charge an application fee to pay for their time. If you closed the loan with them, they'd often use it to pay for the appraisal report or another one of the customary closing costs.

I have always been against charging an application fee to give you a quote. But as of August 2009, the law says you cannot be charged an application fee before you receive a GFE. But it does allow lenders to charge for and pull your credit report first. If you already know your score, don't let that happen. Any loan officer who won't give you a GFE up front—before pulling your credit report and before charging you money—is a loan officer you need to pass on.

Some lenders use the application fee as a decoy. They advertise "no appraisal fee," but then they charge an application fee that pays for the appraisal fee—*whatever!* I think that's insulting and annoying. A fee should state its genuine purpose. If they lie to you about what a certain fee is for, you have to wonder what other lies they have up their sleeves.

A typical application fee is $150 to $400, but don't pay it without seeing the GFE first.

Lender Fee or "Other Fee"

Some lenders brag that they have "no underwriting fee and no processing fee," but then you see something called "lender fee." Helloo, that's the same thing. I find it to be an annoying marketing ploy. And sometimes they call it simply "other fee," whatever that's supposed to mean.

One homebuyer asked the loan officer, "What does the $700 'other fee' pay for?"

The loan officer replied, "That's just for standard closing costs." In other words, she gave him no answer whatsoever and lost his business as a result.

👎 Bad Practice

Accepting all fees on blind faith with no clear explanation.

👍 Good Practice

Understanding your closing costs and what each fee is for. That's how smart homebuyers avoid being taken advantage of.

Third-Party Fees

Third-party fees are for the services performed by outside companies. This money does not go to the lender. Here is the list in alphabetical order.

Appraisal Fee

A licensed appraiser will inspect the property and make a determination on the current value based on the sale of similar homes. This report benefits both you and the lender. You're both investing money in the property and you want to make sure it's not overpriced.

Never pay for an appraisal before you have reviewed and approved the Good Faith Estimate. The appraisal report belongs to the lender, and if you switch companies, you will have to buy a new appraisal report, unless the lender releases it to their competitor. Don't count on that happening.

Per the Home Value Code of Conduct, you have a right to receive a copy of the appraisal report three days before closing, if you have a conventional loan. For other types of loans, including FHA, you have a right to receive a copy at closing. It's a lot of fun to read all the stats about your new home.

Appraisal costs vary by region and according to the type of report ordered, but $400 to $450 is typical. A report for a Jumbo Loan, an investment property, or a duplex can be $600 to $1,000.

Attorney Fee or Escrow/Settlement Fee

Federal regulations require lenders to use a neutral party to close the loan and handle the disbursement of funds. Eastern states use attorneys or title reps. Western states use escrow or title reps.

There can be a significant variation between closing agents. I highly recommend that you call at least two to compare.

Because most people aren't familiar with escrow companies, real estate agents usually end up choosing the closing agent, and like my loan processor said, "Some of these agents choose the most expensive escrow companies!" It's true, and you have to wonder how they make their selection—whether it's by friendship or the exchange of gifts or just very expensive good service.

You can look in your local yellow pages or search Google with your city name + escrow to find companies to call. You might save yourself $200 to $400. I highly favor the escrow companies that charge one all-encompassing fee rather than a fee plus three or four additional fees.

When you call, ask if they charge an "e-mail fee"—that is a pet peeve of mine, and I'd like to rid our industry of that pest. You can read about that in the upcoming section, "Eight Bogus Junk Fees."

If your escrow company or attorney is too far away for you to drive into the office for signing, a mobile notary can come to you for signing. There is a nominal fee for this service, about $150–$250.

Some escrow companies want to charge you a notary fee even if you go into their office, and I think that's plain silly. Signing the loan papers with you is part of what their $400–$900 fee is for, so why do they need to tack on $100 or more for the additional three minutes it takes to plunk their notary stamp on a few pages?

Today I saw a new junk fee pop up on a closing Settlement Statement (the document that shows all the costs of your loan). It said $40 Escrow Archive Fee. I asked the escrow officer what that was for because I'd never seen it before.

Her reply: "It's a new fee for our company and will be charged on ALL files in the future."

Okay then, that really explains what it's for, doesn't it? Clearly, it's a superfluous add-on. Like they need an extra $40 to file the documents in their archive! And like their $873 escrow fee isn't enough to include that task!

👎 Bad Practice

Letting the seller's agent choose a high-priced closing company that tacks on three or four stupid junk fees, in addition to their already high price.

👍 Good Practice

Finding a *good* closing agent ahead of time and designating that company on your proposed purchase and sale agreement. Chances are, the seller will agree with your selection if you ask.

It has become increasingly common for escrow and title companies to add optional fees such as Notary Fee, Courier or Messenger Fee, Wire Fee, Doc Prep Fee, Archive Fee, and whatever else they dream up tomorrow.

For example, for the identical loan, one escrow company charges $795 plus a wire fee and a courier fee and an e-mail fee, and another escrow company charges a flat rate of $490 with no extra fees whatsoever—now that's a company I want to give my business to.

On a refinance, I saw a Fed Ex fee and a courier fee. Were they sending the loan documents back by Fed Ex or by courier? Why two fees? I called the president of the escrow company to ask what was up, and I could hardly believe my ears. He freely told me they were both fees added purely for their escrow company's profit. They'd been getting away with this rip-off for years, because no one ever objected. How infuriating is that?

Once you get to the signing table, it's too late to negotiate these fees, so you have to do your escrow company shopping up front.

Credit Report

Your credit report is ordered from all three bureaus and reviewed to approve your loan. Ask for a copy at closing because it will show your true credit scores from Experian, Equifax, and TransUnion.

Some lenders will cover this cost for you, but it's usually about $15 for an individual and double that for a married couple.

Flood Certification

This determines whether you're in a flood zone and require flood insurance. Most lenders make it mandatory, no matter where you live.

It's only about $12 to $19, so save your complaints for the big stuff.

Tax Service

This is a one-time fee for the service that makes sure your property taxes are paid on time. It protects both you and the lender from the possibility of having your loan slide into default and foreclosure because the taxes weren't paid or posted properly.

It's less than $100.

Title Insurance

You pay only once for the insurance to protect your title for as long as you have the loan. The title company insures you against false liens and judgments, fraud, false affidavits, forged Deeds, unknown heirs, impersonations, and errors. You'd be surprised how often these things come up. Title insurance is extremely important.

The fee varies greatly according to state and loan size, so giving an estimate here is impossible. Your loan officer will estimate on the Good Faith Estimate for you.

If you live in a state that uses escrow companies for closing, you can use one company for both title and escrow. I favor this option because you avoid the possibility of having a $75 subescrow fee (a second escrow fee for the title company to check the escrow company). In a subescrow situation, it can take an extra day to close, possibly throwing off the closing date on your purchase contract.

Recording Fee or Reconveyance Fee

Your local county recorder's office records the Deed of Trust and conveys the recording number to the closing agent. The cost depends on where the property is and how many pages are in the Deed.

In Arizona, $65 is typical. In California, $100. In Boston, $300.

State or City Stamp Tax

If you're in an Eastern state that has this tax as a source of revenue, it's unavoidable.

Survey

In some states, such as Texas, having a survey done on the property is mandatory.

Eight Bogus Junk Fees

This is a pet peeve of mine. I detest needless, unnecessary fees. That's why I, and many other professionals, call them "junk fees" or "garbage fees." Some of them might be small, but they all add up. Some companies purposely sprinkle in four or five of these small fees, counting on you not to object to small numbers, but like I said, they add up. The main reason I want everyone to object to bogus fees is to help clean up the mortgage industry. If a stupid e-mail fee is a deal breaker for enough people and the companies who charge e-mail fees hear enough consumers say, "No, thanks; I'll take my business to a company that doesn't charge to receive the documents by e-mail," then they'll either stop the nonsense or dry up for lack of customers. Either way is fine by me.

In recent years since the subprime mortgage meltdown of 2007, more junk fees have popped up than ever before. If you think that the demise of the subprime lenders took care of the junk, you are wrong as wrong can be. It's worse than ever, and I want homebuyers and homeowners refinancing to insist that it stop now.

Some of the worst offenders are escrow companies. They jumped on the junk fee bandwagon, perhaps after they observed all the lender junk fees. It used to be that all escrow companies were pretty much the same, but that is no longer true. I encourage you to call three escrow companies and ask three questions:

1. What is your fee for a loan amount of $X?
2. Do you charge an e-mail fee? (If they do, make sure you communicate that this is a deal breaker.)
3. Do you charge an extra notary fee, even if I come in to the office to sign?

When homebuyers and homeowners walk away from insane fees, only then will the insanity stop.

Ancillary Fee

The word ancillary means helping. Just who is this fee supposed to help? Certainly not you, as it is totally meaningless when it comes to a mortgage.

Appraisal Review Fee

This used to be common with subprime lenders. If you see it, object. If the underwriter wants a second opinion, let them pay for it, not you. That's part of what their underwriting/administration fee is for.

Doc Prep Fee

Personally, I object to this fee that's popped up in recent years. Preparing the loan documents is part of the job, and it should not require an extra cost. We used to see this on subprime loans only, but now some brokers and even escrow companies are trying to slip it in. I can't think of any other type of business that charges you extra to prepare the contract. They're thrilled to get their paperwork in front of you for your signature, so they can seal the deal. Preparing loan documents is essential to being in the loan business. It's part of the job. You shouldn't have to shell out an additional hundred bucks or more for the paperwork. I've even seen loans where both the lender and the closing agent were charging a doc prep fee. Go figure.

Doc Review Fee

First, they want to charge extra to prepare the documents, and now they want to charge extra again to check them over after you've signed? I don't think so! A staff person reviews all the pages to make sure they're signed properly, and it takes about 15 minutes, give or take. This is a junk fee.

Today I saw this disguised as an "investor review fee." That, too, is bogus.

E-Mail Fee

Are you kidding me? This is the most harebrained fee I've ever heard of. We used to laugh our heads off when this fee popped up on rare occasion, but now more and more companies are trying to slip it in. Closing agents love this stupid junk fee. They claim they need to charge you an extra $50 to $250 because the loan documents were sent to them via e-mail and they had to print them out. Come on, the paper and ink for printing out 50 pages is about $3. That should be absorbed in their big escrow/settlement fee of several hundred dollars.

What if the restaurant you dined at charged you $10 extra for napkins? Would that make you angry? It's the same thing, and that's why I want consumers to say a big "NO WAY" to the e-mail fee. But beware, you have to do it up front. If you wait until you get to the closing table, you're stuck and have no power to get it waived.

Note to Real Estate Agents

Please help us clean up the garbage by objecting to the e-mail fee and archive fee when title and escrow reps solicit you for business. Let them know we want more than their charm: We want fair and decent pricing, too.

Funding Fee

I can't think of one good reason why a lender should charge several hundred additional dollars to fund your loan. They got paid for their administrative/underwriting work, they got paid for processing, and they're making a nice sum on the interest or for selling your loan or on the service release premium. And now some want to pop on an additional $295–$495 to give the green light to the attorney or escrow company to disburse funds? I'm getting depressed just thinking about how that rips off innocent borrowers who have struggled to save enough money to buy a home.

Photo Review Fee

What a laugh! As if the underwriter doesn't automatically look at the photos on the appraisal report without an additional $50.

Satisfaction Fee

Are you kidding me? $125 for whose satisfaction? Certainly not yours.

Is This a Good Faith Estimate or a Joke?

Speaking of "feeing you to death," get a load of this Good Faith Estimate a homebuyer sent to me in November of 2008. Notice the myriad of odd and unusual fees:

Line 819 Loan Acquisition Fee $550

Line 820 Misc. Attorney Charges $ 95

Line 821 Automated U/W Fee $ 20

Line 822 Contract U/W Fee to MGIC $ 85

Line 824 Processing Virgin Money $450

Line 825 MERS Registration/Table Funding $200

Line 1105 Document Preparation Fee $ 32

Line 1112 Municipal Lien Certificate $ 90

Line 1306 Plot Plan $125

Note: This property is in California, where table funding is not allowed (line 825) and where there is no municipal lien certificate (line 1112). And what is processing virgin money? I'd love to hear an explanation for that. But then going down to the bottom, you see out of numeric order, lines 901–1104, the prepaid interest, hazard insurance, and property taxes are all left blank—and yet they are a necessary part of the loan. The borrower told me the closing date was midmonth, and they're having taxes and insurance included in the payment.

Good Faith Estimate with Junk Fees

(not a loan commitment)

Date Prepared: 11/19/2008	Loan Type: 30-Year Fixed	
	Property Type: Single Family	
	Occupancy: Owner Occupied	
Sales Price (Home Value): $400,000	Interest Rate: 6.000%	Amortization: Fully Amortizing
Base Loan Amount: $320,000	Total Loan: $320,000	Documentation: Full Doc
Monthly Principal & Interest Payment: $1,918.56	Est. APR: 6.066%	Prepaid Charges Used in APR calc: $2,239.00

HUD-1	ITEM		AMOUNT
A 801	Origination Due Lender°	0.000 Points	0.00
A 802	Discount°	0.000 Points	0.00
803	Appraisal Fee		300.00
804	Credit Report		19.00
A 805	Lender's Inspection Fee		0.00
A 808	Tax Service Contract		73.00
A 809	Underwriter Review		0.00
A 810	Administration Fee		150.00
A 811	Application Fee		0.00
A 813	Warehouse Fee		0.00
POC 814	Yield Spread Premium	0.000	
A 818	Flood Cert		16.00
A 819	Loan Acquisition Fee		550.00
A 820	Miscellaneous Attorney Charges		95.00
A 821	Automated U/W Fee LP		20.00
A 822	Contract U/W Fee to MGIC		85.00
A 823	Wire/Courier Fee		0.00
A 824	Processing Virgin Money		450.00
A 825	MERS Registration/Table Funding Fee		200.00
A 1101	Settlement or Closing Fee		600.00
1102	Abstract or Title Search Fee		0.00
1103	Title Examination Fee		0.00
1104	Title Insurance Binder		0.00
1105	Document Preparation Fee		32.00
1107	Attorney Fee		0.00
1108	Title Insurance Premium—Lender's Coverage	$800.00	
1108	Title Insurance Premium—Owner's Coverage (optional) $655.00		1455.00
1112	Municipal Lien Certificate		90.00
1201	Recording Fee		300.00
1202	City/County Tax Stamps		0.00
1203	State Tax Stamps		0.00
1204	Intangibles Tax/Doc Stamps		0.00
1301	Survey		0.00
1302	Termite Inspection		0.00
1305	Title Surcharges/Environment Taxes		0.00

1306	Plot Plan	125.00
1307	Recording Fee for Subordination Agreement	0.00
	Total Estimated Closing Costs:	4,560.00
	Lender/Seller Credits:	$0.00
	Estimated Closing Costs after Credits	$4,560.00
	Items required by lender to be paid in advance	
A 901	Prepaid Interest 0 days @ $52.60/Day	0.00
A 902	Mortgage Insurance Premium (If Applicable)	$0/Year (est.)
903	Hazardous Insurance Premium (If Applicable— premium must be paid prior to closing)	$0/Year (est.)
904	Flood Insurance Premium (If Applicable— premium must be paid prior to closing)	$0/Year (est.)
	Reserves deposited with lender	
1001	Hazard Insurance Impounds 2 Months @ $0.00/Month)	0.00
A 1002	Mortgage Insurance Impounds 0 Months @ $0.00/Month)	0.00
1004	Property Tax Impounds 4 Months @ $0.00/Month)	0.00
1006	Flood Insurance Impounds 0 Months @ $0.00/Month)	0.00
	Estimated Prepaid Items/Reserves:	$0.00
	Total Estimated Settlement Charges (Estimated Prepaid Items/ Reserves + Estimated Closing)	$4,560.00
	Total Estimated Funds Needed to Close	$84,560.00

° The Loan Origination or Discount Fee is the amount of the total points or fees paid to FNE.

Closing Costs That Are Not Fees

No, I haven't lost my mind. There are two categories of fees that are neither lender fees nor third-party fees. They are legitimate costs and not bogus junk. You'll see what I mean…

Buying Down Your Interest Rate

Here's how you can get a lower interest rate on your loan: Buy down the rate by paying a sum up front in closing costs.

Loan Origination Fee/Broker Fee

When you opt to pay this fee, you enable yourself to get par rate, the lowest interest rate available without paying extra to buy down the rate. When you pay no percentage points up front, you are opting to take a higher interest rate. No exceptions; that is the way the math works. The reason I say this fee is "not a fee" is because, technically, it is interest you're paying up front to get a lower interest rate for the life of the loan. That is why this fee is income tax deductible—because it is interest, just like the interest portion of your monthly payment, which is also income tax deductible. (Consult your tax accountant for details. Typically, on a purchase loan, you can deduct the entire fee in the first year; and on a refinance, it is tax deductible over the years of the loan.)

Warning

On the new, proposed Good Faith Estimate form designed by government people for 2010 and beyond, it says: "Our origination charge. This charge is for getting this loan for you." That is misleading. It sounds like it's a lender fee or a broker fee and not up-front interest. It gives the impression it would be best to pay zero, which is not true most of the time. It opens a door for lenders to brag about "no origination charge" and not explain that you pay more with a higher rate and monthly payment *forever* because of it.

Also, this new GFE form doesn't have a space designated for the Discount Fee, explained in the next section. I don't like that because you can't clearly and easily see how much extra you're paying to get a lower rate than par.

Discount Fee

If you want to buy down your rate lower than the par rate, you do so by paying additional interest up front in the form of the Discount Fee.

If your loan has an additional cost required by the National Federal Mortgage Association (Fannie Mae), such as the property is a condo/townhome, you opt not to have taxes and insurance included in your payment, you are doing a cash-out refinance at a higher loan-to-value ratio, or your credit score is low, then the additional fee might be shown here.

Beware of sly loan officers who purport to have no Origination Fee, but then give you a Discount Fee instead. The Discount Fee is supposed to be for *something extra*, not for camouflaging the Origination Fee.

Prepaids and Reserves

These closing costs are not fees paid for anyone's profit, but they are closing costs that are a part of a mortgage.

Prepaid Interest or Daily Interest Charge

From the date your loan closes through the last day of the month, you pay interest. If your loan closes on the last day of the month, it will be one day. It is exactly fair. Also, notice when your first payment is due. If your loan closes mid-January, your first payment will be due March 1. You skip February because mortgage payments are made in arrears. (You live there first, and then pay for the month—just the opposite of renting where you pay first and then live there.)

Beware if the prepaid interest is left blank. You'll probably be in for a surprise at closing, unless your loan funds at the beginning of the month and you don't skip a month ahead to start your first payment.

Reserves

These are not lender fees. These are the estimated property taxes and homeowner's (fire) insurance premium that is collected up front. How many months' property taxes are required depends on the tax payment cycle and what month your loan closes. This figure will be the same, no matter which lender you work with.

Coming Up Next

If you don't understand Yield Spread Premium, you could be bilked out of tens of thousands of dollars. No homebuyer can afford to be without this knowledge, coming up next.

15

Five Things You Need to Know About YSP

It's been called the best-kept secret in the mortgage business. Trying to get a banker to talk about it is like trying to pry a secret out of the FBI. If they say anything at all, it's going to be a cover-up. And the worst part is: This is costing homebuyers tens of thousands of dollars over the life of the loan. What am I talking about?

It's an important part of your financing, called Yield Spread Premium (YSP). One afternoon, a loan officer treated me to a filet-mignon lunch at the upscale Daniel's Broiler overlooking Lake Washington and the Seattle skyline beyond. While we were dining, he boasted of making 40 grand in commission on one loan. How? With the Yield Spread Premium.

Another loan officer posted on a public forum that he attracts clients by charging only half a percent Origination Fee rather than the standard 1 percent; but then he went on to say he actually makes three times that amount per loan. How? With the Yield Spread Premium.

I knew a young female loan officer who regularly made 5 percent on every loan she did. How? By charging "two up front and three on the back end." That means she charged 1 percent Origination Fee, 1 percent Discount Fee, and got a 3 percent Yield Spread Premium. I call that taking advantage, and here's what you need to know so you can avoid having something like that happen to you.

What Is Yield Spread Premium?

Yield Spread Premium (YSP) is money, a premium, paid to the mortgage broker for selling a loan that has a higher interest rate than par rate. It is also written as POC (Paid Outside Closing). On the new proposed Good Faith Estimate, they're going to list it on page 2 as a "credit."

You see, every day there is a par rate. It's the lowest rate of the day you can get without paying an extra Discount Fee. A new par rate is posted every morning, and on some days, it changes two or three times during the day as well. (Each wholesale lender or wholesale division of a bank posts their rates daily, but to get access, you have to be a mortgage broker with a confirmed account and password. These rates are not available to the public, so you have to ask your mortgage broker to find out.)

When the mortgage broker gives you a loan at par rate, the wholesale lender who is backing the loan does not pay him any extra money outside of closing. But when the mortgage broker gives you a loan with a higher interest rate, the wholesale lender will make more money, so they share the profit by paying the broker a premium called Yield Spread Premium, paid outside of closing.

Yield Spread Premium can also be earned by placing a higher margin on an adjustable rate mortgage. That was common with the infamous Option ARM loan, also popularly called pick-a-payment loan. The low teaser rate was enticing, but once that high margin kicked in and the rate skyrocketed, tens of thousands of homeowners were booted out of their no-longer-affordable homes as banks foreclosed.

Is YSP a Rip-Off to Borrowers?

There is nothing wrong or evil about a Yield Spread Premium, per se. In fact, there are times when *you* can use it to your own advantage, as explained in Chapter 16, "How the YSP Controversy Affects You." My objection comes when unscrupulous loan officers overcharge and hide it from you so that you never know. A modest

YSP to the mortgage broker is not a rip-off, but a hidden, high YSP certainly is.

If your loan is $400,000 and you pay one point (1 percent Origination Fee), you assume you are getting a fair deal. But if there's a hidden 2 percent YSP, you're being overcharged and ripped off. So, always ask if you don't see it on your Good Faith Estimate.

☞ Bad Practice

Freaking out over seeing a YSP on your Good Faith Estimate and HUD-1 Settlement Statement.

👍 Good Practice

Understanding that a YSP figure that is a small fraction of your loan amount is fair and customary. Banks also have overages; they just don't have to disclose it.

Lenders That Don't Have YSP

You've just read that when a mortgage broker gives you a higher interest rate than the par rate, the wholesale lender with the money backing the loan pays the broker a premium. But what happens if you go to a bank or a lending company that uses its own money rather than the money from an outside wholesale lender?

There is no premium money paid from wholesaler to broker when the lender is using their own money. To put it another way, there is no transfer of funds from one company to another because only one company is involved. Therefore, there is no YSP.

Nonetheless, a bank has their daily par rate and rates above and below par. A loan officer at a bank or direct lender can give you a loan with an interest rate above par and make extra money—it's just that they don't call it YSP. They might call it an "overage." They might have a Service Release Premium instead of a Yield Spread Premium. That is extremely common.

Federal law requires mortgage brokers to disclose their YSP on the Good Faith Estimate. Now here's the unfair part: Federal law does not require banks or direct lenders using their own money to disclose their "overage" or to disclose their Service Release Premium. They don't have to breathe a word about it. The overage or SRP is their big, fat, hidden secret.

Clearly, banks and direct lenders are not held to the same standards for transparency that mortgage brokers are. So keep that in mind when you ask the two following pertinent questions.

Two Intelligent Questions You Should Ask

I recommend asking these two questions when you receive your Good Faith Estimate if the YSP is not clearly spelled out.

1. Ask: "What is the YSP or overage on my loan?"

   Be sure to use those exact words because if you just ask what the YSP is, a lender who is using their own money will say, "We don't have YSP." Technically, that's true, and you'll never find out the overage if you don't ask. Even though a lender using their own money isn't required to tell you their overage, it's not illegal for them to tell you either. So ask and see what kind of an answer you get. If they dance all around the subject and say they don't have YSP and that is why they're "cheaper" and refuse to address the overage, then you know they do have an overage, but they're hiding it. On the other hand, if the loan officer says something like, "Good question. This is par rate today and there is no YSP or overage," then you can feel good and proceed with that mortgage star. Or, if they say, "We don't have YSP, but there is a small overage of less than $500," then you can feel great that you're talking with an honest professional and you should proceed with confidence with that mortgage star.

2. Ask: "What is par rate today?"

   Depending on the first answer you get, you might or might not need to ask this second question. But before you do, finish this chapter and the next one because having only a partial understanding about how rates and YSP work can lead you into a misunderstanding. For example, if the loan officer says, "There is no exact par rate today," he is not giving you the runaround. That will be explained in a moment.

Make Sure You Get a Choice

Ask your loan officer to give you a couple choices for interest rate versus Origination Fee. That way, you'll make an informed decision and feel good about having the best loan for your situation.

Here's an example for a $200,000 loan:

Choice #1: Standard	Choice #2: Pay Less Up Front, Higher Rate
1% Origination Fee ($2,000)	.5% Origination Fee ($1,000)
5.75% rate	6.125% rate
$1,167/mo.	$1,215/mo.

I am a strong believer in giving people options because it's your home and you should be the one to decide on the best financing choice for you. I super hate it when a loan officer dictates a rate with zero Origination Fee without giving the borrower a choice of having a lower rate. Now on to five things you need to know about your financing.

Five Important Principles to Understanding YSP

It's easy to understand how the Yield Spread Premium works when you grasp these five simple facts. Even if you're the right-brain, artistic type, you can "get it" and understand your mortgage:

1. YSP is directly tied to the interest rate.
2. The higher the rate, the larger the YSP.
3. Par rate means there is no YSP.
4. Some days, there is no exact par rate.
5. No consistent formula exists for calculating the YSP.

Let's explore these five principles a little more to see how this information can help you choose the best financing.

👎 **Bad Practice**

Doing business with dishonest loan officers. When something doesn't feel right, listen to your gut instinct and ask questions. If you don't get clear answers, that loan officer is not for you.

👍 **Good Practice**

Doing your part to clean up the mortgage industry by giving your business to honest loan officers. If everyone does this, the liars and sharks will be forced to clean up their act or go out of business.

---

1 & 2. YSP is directly tied to the interest rate; and the higher the rate, the larger the YSP.

It is helpful to know that YSP is tied to the interest rate when you're comparing two GFEs where the YSP is not disclosed. Logically, this goes right along with the second principle, the higher the rate, the larger the YSP. As long as both GFEs have the same charge for Origination/Broker Fee, you can compare the interest rate for an apples-to-apples comparison.

For example:

Mars Mortgage	Venus Mortgage
1% Origination Fee	1% Origination Fee
5.625%	5.75%
$1,000 YSP	YSP not disclosed

You don't have to be confused about Venus Mortgage not disclosing their YSP. You see that Mars Mortgage is making $1,000 YSP with a 5.625 percent rate, so now you know the YSP for Venus Mortgage is higher than that because the interest rate is one-eighth higher. Clearly, Mars Mortgage has the cheaper loan. Just make sure Mars Mortgage doesn't have exorbitant or a myriad of junk fees to offset it.

3. Par rate is the lowest rate you can get without paying any extra Discount Fee to buy down the rate.

At par rate, the mortgage brokers do not get paid any extra money for selling a higher rate than par; therefore, there must be an up-front Origination/Broker Fee for them to get paid. If your loan has zero Origination/Broker Fee, you are not getting par rate. If a loan officer tells you the rate is at par with zero points, you know you're talking to a liar because no one works for free. In that case, I recommend bidding that person farewell and rewarding an honest loan officer with your business instead. That's how the American people can show their power, and that's how the dirty side of lending is cleaned up organically, without federal laws.

4. Some days there is no exact par with a zero YSP. For example, today I'm looking at a rate sheet that looks like this:

Interest Rate	Yield Spread Premium
5.125%	<.25> YSP
5 %	<.125> YSP
4.875%	Cost of .5

To apply this information on a loan of $300,000:

$300,000 loan @ 5.125% → $750 YSP

$300,000 loan @ 5 %   → $375 YSP

$300,000 loan @ 4.875% → Extra cost of $1,500 to borrower

For this particular lender today, there is no exact par rate. The closest rate to par is 5 percent. Do not freak out about the mortgage broker making a little extra; remember, the loan officer has to split that with the company anyway. It's no big deal. It is fair and reasonable for a loan officer to make $2,000–$3,000 on average per loan. (They would expect to make more on a Jumbo Loan or a difficult loan requiring extra work and time.)

5. No consistent formula exists for calculating YSP.

If a formula existed, I would include it here; but, unfortunately, the ratio varies wildly and changes every day. For example, I'm going to use the same rate sheet I quoted from previously, but I'm going to expand it so you can clearly see the numeric inconsistency.

Notice that the interest rates are in one-eighth (.125) increments, but the YSP or extra cost is not proportionate. Rates of 5.25 percent and 5.125 percent have the same YSP of .25, which seems to make no sense. And the cost of getting 4.25 percent is disproportionately high, showing the investor really doesn't want to give you that rate.

Look at the following chart and you'll see what I mean. But then you also need to understand that this is *just for today*. Tomorrow, the proportions will be entirely different. There might be an exact 0 YSP par rate, and there is likely to be a significant difference between 5.25 percent and 5.125 percent.

Interest Rate	Yield Spread Premium	Comment
5.25%	<.25> YSP	**The lender makes no more on 5.25 than on 5.125 today.**
5.125%	<.25> YSP	
5 %	<.125> YSP	**A small difference for 1/8 better rate here.**
4.875%	Cost of .5	**A large difference of 5/8 fee for 1/8 better here!**
4.75%	Cost of .625	**A small difference for 1/8 better rate here.**
4.625%	Cost of 1	**A Discount Fee of 1% to get this rate today.**
4.5%	Cost of 1.375	
4.375%	Cost of 1.75	
4.25%	Cost of 2.375	**Wow, look how much more it costs to get 4.25 today than to get 4.5: an extra 1% fee.**

Don't let this information throw you for a loop. The only thing you need to concern yourself with to get an awesome, cheap loan is comparing the interest rate and the Origination/Broker Fee. If the YSP is properly disclosed, great. If the YSP is minor (a small percentage of your loan amount), you know there wasn't an exact par that day, and it was the lowest rate the loan officer could give you without charging an extra Discount Fee to buy down the rate. That's fine. You now know that a Yield Spread Premium is not a rip-off, providing it isn't a ridiculously high figure.

The YSP chart might be complex, but it is simple to get a great loan when you follow my method of comparing Good Faith Estimates.

Coming Up Next

Some lawmakers are doing their darned best to make getting a mortgage more difficult and more unfair. Their proposed laws are sheer idiocy, and you have the right to know what's going on. The controversy is explained in the next chapter.

16

How the YSP Controversy Affects You

Let's say you're house hunting and you find an outdated, ugly house offered at an attractive price. You'll need some cash to clean it up, paint, and replace the stained carpets; but once that's done, you can resell at a profit. What is your best loan in this situation?

You'll want to opt for no Origination Fee and take the higher interest rate, instead of buying down the rate with an Origination Fee. Why? Because you want to save your cash to fix up the house—and because you're not going to keep the house long enough to justify buying down the rate by paying the Origination Fee. But get this…

The federal government—spurred by certain politicians with more hubris than mortgage smarts—wants to deny you the right to take a no–Origination Fee loan. That's right. They're demanding that the mortgage broker be paid up front and cannot take a commission via Yield Spread Premium. They're pushing for a law that says any Yield Spread Premium has to be credited back to the borrower.

👎 Bad Practice

Automatically taking whatever loan the lender puts in front of you.

👍 Good Practice

Looking at options. You can pay zero points and take a higher interest rate, or you can pay a point and get a lower interest rate. A third option is buying down the rate below par.

That really steams me! How dare they pass a law denying you the right to choose whether you want to pay an Origination Fee or take a higher rate?

It's an insane idea that hurts borrowers. Without the law, loan officers are allowed to credit some or all of the Yield Spread Premium they receive to the borrower—and they do so when the situation warrants it. But requiring it in every situation is a kick in the shins to borrowers because it forces them to pay an Origination/Broker Fee.

Not only that, but it hurts first-time homebuyers and low-to-middle income borrowers the most. Those are the folks with the least amount of cash to pay closing costs. It's hard enough saving for a down payment! Why shouldn't they be able to take a zero Origination/Broker Fee loan and let the mortgage broker get paid by YSP?

But wait, it gets worse.

The law says mortgage brokers can't get paid from a Yield Spread Premium; and yet, there are homebuyers who need and want a zero Origination Fee loan. Because they can't get it from a mortgage broker, they have no choice but to go to a bank to get it.

This, in turn, strips a giant portion of business away from mortgage brokers—and voila!—the banks get to ditch their competition that prevented them from charging homebuyers too much. As we all know, competition is good for consumers; competition drives down prices. But now with the law preventing mortgage brokers from offering no–Origination Fee loans, the banks can raise rates higher and pocket bigger profits. The banks win and the two losers are the mortgage brokers and you, the homebuyer.

👎 **Bad Practice**

Naively believing that every new law passed by the government is in the homebuyers' favor.

👍 **Good Practice**

Writing to your Congress representative to express your desire to have a choice; and that one of the choices you want to be given is the ability to let the loan officer get paid via Yield Spread Premium if you don't want to pay an up-front Origination Fee/Broker Fee.

Is this fair? Is this in the best interest of the public? Does this help homebuyers? Does it create a level playing field between bankers and brokers? Absolutely not! And that's why I think it is sheer idiocy to make it illegal for mortgage brokers to get paid by the overage (or Yield Spread Premium) when the banks do it all day long.

Instructions to Lie

My first job in the mortgage business was with a huge, successful national lender. The company was rich and had its own money to lend, like a bank. In training, I was taught to tell customers that they could get a cheaper loan with us than they could get with a mortgage broker because "mortgage brokers are a middleman."

"You save money with us because we're the lender," we were instructed to say.

It took longer than it should have for me to discover that it was a boldface lie because they also had another cardinal rule—*and what a rule it was!*

👎 Bad Practice

Profiling all mortgage brokers as being dishonest and greedy. That is ignorance in action.

👍 Good Practice

Being aware that there are good, honest mortgage brokers and there are good, honest bankers.

Also being aware that there are dishonest, greedy mortgage brokers and there are dishonest, greedy bankers.

An intelligent person does not profile a career any more than they profile a race.

Like a cult that doesn't allow their members to interact with the outside world, our manager told us it was company policy that we were not allowed to communicate with mortgage brokers—and that if we did, we would be INSTANTLY FIRED!

"Why is that?" we asked.

"Because that's company policy," our manager repeated. And that was it. If we valued having a paycheck, then we were to have nothing to do with those evil mortgage brokers—those horrid middlemen. Later, I discovered the real reason behind the policy. It was because the mortgage brokers undersold us by so much—their loans were so much cheaper—it was a total and complete embarrassment. I remember feeling horrified when I learned the truth. It was almost like Paul on the Road to Damascus who heard God's voice in a bright, shining light.

It was a real lightbulb moment all right.

I began referring people to a certain mortgage broker I came to know. He was a good guy who offered cheap loans, and I couldn't bring myself to charge people who had excellent credit more when he could help them for less.

This didn't go on for very long. Shortly, I gave my notice and became a mortgage broker myself. From then on, I enjoyed the satisfaction of closing good, cheap loans for all my wonderful homebuyers. I was able to give people lower interest rates because as the so-called middleman, I was able to go to the wholesale lending divisions and save people tens of thousands of dollars.

So don't fall for the old line, "We save you money because we're a bank or direct lender, and we don't have Yield Spread Premium." Maybe they'll save you money and maybe they won't. It depends a lot on the individual loan officer. At most lending institutions, loan officers have the freedom to price their loans as they want—within certain parameters, of course. Read the Good Faith Estimate to find out.

The Fight Is Coming to Blows

As I sit at my desk writing, the National Association of Mortgage Brokers has filed a lawsuit against the federal government because of this damaging, unfair law requiring mortgage brokers, but not bankers, to credit all their overage (YSP) to the borrower.

By the time you hold this book in your hands, the lawsuit might be settled. If the brokers win, the homebuyers also win. If the new law prevails, I hope every homebuyer and homeowner calls in a protest to their state representatives in an attempt to overturn this abomination. Clearly, Yield Spread Premium should not be outlawed, and it should not be mandatory to credit it back to the borrower.

Coming Up Next

"Seven Ways They Can Trick You on the Good Faith Estimate," (in Chapter 17) is not to be missed! This is insider information you won't find elsewhere, and it will put you ahead of the game, so no one can pull a fast one and take advantage of your pocketbook.

17

The Good Faith Estimate: Tricks and Traps

Comparing Good Faith Estimates (GFEs) can be like judging a contest between a mango, a plum, and a peach. Although most mortgage brokers use a standard one-page GFE form, banks and direct lenders often use their own creative forms. Some of these forms omit essential fees, some hide the interest rate, and some don't even disclose your monthly payment. Now how are you supposed to make an informed decision based on that confusion?

This perplexity caused the U.S. Department of Housing and Urban Development (HUD) to create a new Good Faith Estimate form to be used by brokers and bankers alike, starting in 2010—that is the proposal at this time.

Let's look at seven tricks lenders use to fool you into thinking their loan is better than it is. Let's look at both the Good Faith Estimate form commonly used by mortgage brokers and the new proposed form, which is also a trap waiting to ensnare unsuspecting citizens. Please see the old and new GFE forms; that way, you will better understand the explanations here.

OMB Approval No. 2502-0265

Good Faith Estimate (GFE)

Name of Originator	Borrower
Originator Address	Property Address
Originator Phone Number	
Originator Email	Date of GFE

Purpose

This GFE gives you an estimate of your settlement charges and loan terms if you are approved for this loan. For more information, see HUD's *Special Information Booklet* on settlement charges, your *Truth-in-Lending Disclosures,* and other consumer information at www.hud.gov/respa. If you decide you would like to proceed with this loan, contact us.

Shopping for your loan

Only you can shop for the best loan for you. Compare this GFE with other loan offers, so you can find the best loan. Use the shopping chart on page 3 to compare all the offers you receive.

Important dates

1. The interest rate for this GFE is available through _____ . After this time, the interest rate, some of your loan Origination Charges, and the monthly payment shown below can change until you lock your interest rate.

2. This estimate for all other settlement charges is available through _____ .

3. After you lock your interest rate, you must go to settlement within ☐ days (your rate lock period) to receive the locked interest rate.

4. You must lock the interest rate at least ☐ days before settlement.

Summary of your loan

Your initial loan amount is	$
Your loan term is	years
Your initial interest rate is	%
Your initial monthly amount owed for principal, interest, and any mortgage insurance is	$ per month
Can your interest rate rise?	☐ No ☐ Yes, it can rise to a maximum of %. The first change will be in .
Even if you make payments on time, can your loan balance rise?	☐ No ☐ Yes, it can rise to a maximum of $
Even if you make payments on time, can your monthly amount owed for principal, interest, and any mortgage insurance rise?	☐ No ☐ Yes, the first increase can be in and the monthly amount owed can rise to $. The maximum it can ever rise to is $.
Does your loan have a prepayment penalty?	☐ No ☐ Yes, your maximum prepayment penalty is $.
Does your loan have a balloon payment?	☐ No ☐ Yes, you have a balloon payment of $ due in years.

Escrow account information

Some lenders require an escrow account to hold funds for paying property taxes or other property-related charges in addition to your monthly amount owed of $ _____ .

Do we require you to have an escrow account for your loan?

☐ No, you do not have an escrow account. You must pay these charges directly when due.

☐ Yes, you have an escrow account. It may or may not cover all of these charges. Ask us.

Summary of your settlement charges

A	Your Adjusted Origination Charges *(See page 2.)*	$
B	Your Charges for All Other Settlement Services *(See page 2.)*	$
A + **B**	Total Estimated Settlement Charges	$

Good Faith Estimate (HUD-GFE) 1

Figure 17.1   The new proposed Good Faith Estimate.

Understanding your estimated settlement charges

Your Adjusted Origination Charges	
1. Our origination charge This charge is for getting this loan for you.	
2. Your credit or charge (points) for the specific interest rate chosen ☐ The credit or charge for the interest rate of ☐ % is included in "Our origination charge." (See item 1 above.) ☐ You receive a credit of $☐ for this interest rate of ☐ %. This credit **reduces** your settlement charges. ☐ You pay a charge of $☐ for this interest rate of ☐ %. This charge (points) **increases** your total settlement charges The tradeoff table on page 3 shows that you can change your total settlement charges by choosing a different interest rate for this loan.	
A Your Adjusted Origination Charges	$

Your Charges for All Other Settlement Services	*Some of these charges can change at settlement. See the top of page 3 for more information.*
3. Required services that we select These charges are for services we require to complete your settlement. We will choose the providers of these services. *Service* *Charge*	
4. Title services and lender's title insurance This charge includes the services of a title or settlement agent, for example, and title insurance to protect the lender, if required.	
5. Owner's title insurance You may purchase an owner's title insurance policy to protect your interest in the property.	
6. Required services that you can shop for These charges are for other services that are required to complete your settlement. We can identify providers of these services or you can shop for them yourself. Our estimates for providing these services are below. *Service* *Charge*	
7. Government recording charges These charges are for state and local fees to record your loan and title documents.	
8. Transfer taxes These charges are for state and local fees on mortgages and home sales.	
9. Initial deposit for your escrow account This charge is held in an escrow account to pay future recurring charges on your property and includes ☐ all property taxes, ☐ all insurance, and ☐ other ☐ .	
10. Daily interest charges This charge is for the daily interest on your loan from the day of your settlement until the first day of the next month or the first day of your normal mortgage payment cycle. This amount is $☐ per day for ☐ days (if your settlement is ☐).	
11. Homeowner's insurance This charge is for the insurance you must buy for the property to protect from a loss, such as fire. *Policy* *Charge*	
B Your Charges for All Other Settlement Services	$
A + **B** Total Estimated Settlement Charges	$

Good Faith Estimate (HUD-GFE) 2

Figure 17.1 Continued

Instructions

Understanding which charges can change at settlement

This GFE estimates your settlement charges. At your settlement, you will receive a HUD-1, a form that lists your actual costs. Compare the charges on the HUD-1 with the charges on this GFE. Charges can change if you select your own provider and do not use the companies we identify. (See below for details.)

These charges **cannot increase** at settlement:	The total of these charges **can increase up to 10%** at settlement:	These charges **can change** at settlement:
■ Our origination charge ■ Your credit or charge (points) for the specific interest rate chosen *(after you lock in your interest rate)* ■ Your adjusted origination charges *(after you lock in your interest rate)* ■ Transfer taxes	■ Required services that we select ■ Title services and lender's title insurance *(if we select them or you use companies we identify)* ■ Owner's title insurance *(if you use companies we identify)* ■ Required services that you can shop for *(if you use companies we identify)* ■ Government recording charges	■ Required services that you can shop for *(if you do not use companies we identify)* ■ Title services and lender's title insurance *(if you do not use companies we identify)* ■ Owner's title insurance *(if you do not use companies we identify)* ■ Initial deposit for your escrow account ■ Daily interest charges ■ Homeowner's insurance

Using the tradeoff table

In this GFE, we offered you this loan with a particular interest rate and estimated settlement charges. However:
- If you want to choose this same loan with **lower settlement charges,** then you will have a **higher interest rate.**
- If you want to choose this same loan with a **lower interest rate,** then you will have **higher settlement charges.**

If you would like to choose an available option, you must ask us for a new GFE.

Loan originators have the option to complete this table. Please ask us for additional information if the table is not completed.

	The loan in this GFE	The same loan with lower settlement charges	The same loan with a lower interest rate
Your initial loan amount	$	$	$
Your initial interest rate [1]	%	%	%
Your initial monthly amount owed	$	$	$
Change in the monthly amount owed from this GFE	No change	You will pay $ **more** every month	You will pay $ **less** every month
Change in the amount you will pay at settlement with this interest rate	No change	Your settlement charges will be **reduced** by $	Your settlement charges will **increase** by $
How much your total estimated settlement charges will be	$	$	$

[1] *For an adjustable rate loan, the comparisons above are for the initial interest rate before adjustments are made.*

Using the shopping chart

Use this chart to compare GFEs from different loan originators. Fill in the information by using a different column for each GFE you receive. By comparing loan offers, you can shop for the best loan.

	This loan	Loan 2	Loan 3	Loan 4
Loan originator name				
Initial loan amount				
Loan term				
Initial interest rate				
Initial monthly amount owed				
Rate lock period				
Can interest rate rise?				
Can loan balance rise?				
Can monthly amount owed rise?				
Prepayment penalty?				
Balloon payment?				
Total Estimated Settlement Charges				

If your loan is sold in the future

Some lenders may sell your loan after settlement. Any fees lenders receive in the future cannot change the loan you receive or the charges you paid at settlement.

 Good Faith Estimate (HUD-GFE) 3

Figure 17.1   Continued

GOOD FAITH ESTIMATE

Applicants: Sample	Application No: Sample
Property Addr:	Date Prepared: 06/04/2009
Prepared By: Carolyn Warren	Loan Program: Conventional, 30-year
Shelter Mortgage/Guaranty Bank	fixed rate

The information provided below reflects estimates of the charges which you are likely to incur at the settlement of your loan. The fees listed are estimates—actual charges may be more or less. Your transaction may not involve a fee for every item listed. The numbers listed beside the estimates generally correspond to the numbered lines contained on the HUD-1 settlement statement that you will be receiving at settlement. The HUD-1 settlement statement will show you the actual cost for items paid at settlement.

Total Loan Amount $_____ Interest Rate_____%_____Term:_____mths

800	**ITEMS PAYABLE IN CONNECTION WITH LOAN:**	**PFC S F POC**
801	Loan Origination Fee	
802	Loan Discount	
803	Appraisal Fee	
804	Credit Report	
805	Lender's Inspection Fee	
808	Mortgage Broker Fee	
809	Tax-Related Service Fee	
810	Processing Fee	
811	Underwriting Fee	
812	Wire Transfer Fee	

1100	**TITLE CHARGES:**	**PFC S F POC**
1101	Closing or Escrow Fee	
1105	Document Preparation Fee	
1106	Notary Fees	
1107	Attorney Fees	
1108	Title Insurance	

1200	**Government Recording & Transfer Charges**	**PFC S F POC**
1201	Recording Fees:	
1202	City/County Tax/Stamps	
1203	State Tax/Stamps	

Figure 17.2 Current Good Faith Estimate.

1300	**ADDITIONAL SETTLEMENT CHARGES**	PFC S F POC
1302	Pest Inspection	

Estimated Closing Costs

900	**ITEMS REQUIRED BY LENDER TO BE PAID IN ADVANCE**	PFC S F POC
901	Interest for days @ $ per day	
902	Mortgage Insurance Premium	
903	Hazard Insurance Premium	
904		
905	VA Funding Fee	

1000	**RESERVES DEPOSITED WITH LENDER**	PFC S F POC
1001	Hazard Insurance Premium months @ $ per month	
1002	Mortgage Ins. Premium Reserves months @ $ per month	
1003	School Tax months @ $ per month	
1004	Taxes and Assessment Reserves months @ $ per month	
1005	Flood Insurance Reserves months @ $ per month	

Estimated Prepaid Items/Reserves

TOTAL ESTIMATED SETTLEMENT CHARGES

COMPENSATION TO BROKER (Not Paid Out of Loan Proceeds)

Yield Spread Premium $

TOTAL ESTIMATED FUNDS NEEDED TO CLOSE:		**TOTAL ESTIMATED MONTHLY PAYMENT:**
Purchase Price/Payoff (+)		New First Mortgage (-) Principal & Interest
Loan Amount (-)	0.00	Sub Financing (-) Other Financing (P&I)
Est. Closing Costs (+)	0.00	New 2nd Mtg Hazard Insurance
		Closing Costs (+)
Est. Prepaid Items/Reserves (+)	0.00	Real Estate Taxes
Amount Paid by Seller (-)		Mortgage Insurance
		Homeowner Assn. Dues
		Other
Total Est. Funds Needed to Close	0.00	**Total Monthly Payment**

Figure 17.2   Continued

This Good Faith Estimate is being provided by Carolyn Warren, a mortgage broker, and no lender has been obtained. **These estimates are provided pursuant to the Real Estate Settlement Procedures Act of 1974, as amended (RESPA). Additional information can be found in the HUD Special Information Booklet, which is to be provided to you by your mortgage broker or lender, if your application is to purchase residential real property and the lender will take a first lien on the property.** The undersigned acknowledge receipt of the booklet, "Settlement Costs," and if applicable, the Consumer Handbook on ARM Mortgages.

Applicant **Sample**   Date Applicant   Date

Figure 17.2   Continued

Seven Ways They Can Trick You on the Good Faith Estimate

There are more tricks to take your money than there are apes in a zoo. Here's some of the monkey business going on now, seven ways loan officers can make their Good Faith Estimates appear to be better than they actually are.

1. Charging a Discount Fee when there is no Origination Fee or Broker Fee.

   Remember, the Origination Fee and Broker Fee are the same thing: interest you're paying up front to get par rate or at least a rate close to par. Banks and direct lenders call it an Origination Fee and brokers call it a Broker Fee.

   A Discount Fee is for buying down the rate below par. If there is no Origination or Broker Fee, then how could there be an extra discount? It makes no sense, but some shady loan officers will tell you there is no Origination Fee in an attempt to make you think you're getting a cheaper deal. If you see this ploy, call them on it to send a message that they're not fooling everybody; and then walk away.

   On the new GFE, you'll see at the top of page 2, #1 "Our origination charge." Then right below it, #2 has three boxes:

   The first box is a blend of Origination Fee and YSP or "credit."

   The second box is for the YSP or "credit."

The third box is for the Discount Fee when you choose to buy down your rate below par.

Beware of #1 "Our origination charge" being left blank or with a 0. And then under #2, third box with $___ filled in. That smells like deception.

2. No appraisal fee.

Unless you have an uncommon situation, such as an FHA streamline refinance (only for homeowners who already have an FHA loan) or a small Home Equity Line of Credit or are getting an exemption (which is unusual and would be unknown until after your approval), there will be an appraisal done by an independent appraiser to determine the current value of your property. The appraiser must be paid for his or her work. If the loan officer tells you they are paying for the appraisal for you, you can be sure you are being charged for it in disguise. One bank might call it an *application fee*; another might call it *lender fees*; and another might call it *miscellaneous*. Or worse, they might pay for it out of their Yield Spread Premium without out letting you know you're taking a higher interest rate to pay for it—and then some!

On the new GFE, the appraisal fee is missing, so the loan officer has to manually add it on page 2, #3 "Required services that we select."

👎 Bad Practice

Naively thinking you're getting "a deal" when the Good Faith Estimate doesn't show fees for mandatory services.

👍 Good Practice

Asking the loan officer what the missing costs are because you don't need to be surprised later. Then ask if you can have a lower interest rate if you pay for them yourself.

3. Mandatory costs left blank.

When unavoidable costs are left blank, it means one of two things. Either you are paying for it out of their secret Yield Spread Premium, or you're going to be surprised with more fees than you were prepared for at closing.

On the new GFE, these should all be listed on page 2 and added up for "Box B." Here are examples of required services that someone has to pay for that might be omitted on your GFE. Some loan officers leave these blank initially, which makes your total settlement charges look lower than they actually are:

a. Closing/Settlement/Escrow Fee

Federal regulations require an independent escrow company or an attorney to close your loan and handle the disbursement of funds. The escrow agent or attorney must be paid.

b. Recording Fee

This is charged by the local County Recorders Office for making a record of your Deed of Trust.

c. Taxes

Some states, particularly in the East, require city/state taxes.

d. Tax Service

Most lenders require a Tax Service Fee of about $75 to $95.

Now back to more tricks...

4. Yield Spread Premium stated as a range.

According to federal regulations, the Yield Spread Premium (YSP) is to be estimated and disclosed clearly in a dollar amount. And yet, the majority of mortgage brokers are putting something like "0%–4%." That tells you nothing! You don't know whether you're getting par rate or if the loan officer has jacked up your rate and is making an extra ten grand. This is not the sign of a mortgage star.

On the new GFE, look for this on page 2, #2 "credit."

5. Yield Spread Premium is nowhere to be found.

Equally aggravating is when mortgage brokers fail to disclose their YSP at all. And bankers, who are not required by law to disclose any YSP, don't help matters. It's an unfair law that makes for an uneven playing field.

I favor a loan officer who shows the YSP right up front on the Good Faith Estimate over those who do not, every time. Remember, having a YSP is not necessarily a bad thing, and it should be disclosed.

6. Prepaid interest omitted.

Unless you close on the first of the month, you will have prepaid interest.

If you close on the very last day of the month, you will have one day of prepaid interest. Most loans have more than zero to one day of prepaid interest, and a reasonable estimate should be on your GFE. In my opinion, 20 days down to 10 days is reasonable.

For example, if you close on January 10, you will own your new house for 20 days in January; thus, you'd pay for 20 days prepaid interest. It's calculated to the day to be precisely fair.

One of the ways sneaky loan officers make their GFEs appear to be cheaper than they are is to leave off or grossly underestimate the days of prepaid interest. In actuality, that number will be identical with every lender (as long as the interest rates are also identical).

On the new GFE, this is on page 2, #10.

7. Seller contribution predicted.

Another trick a loan officer can pull is to subtract five or ten thousand dollars from your closing costs by saying the seller is going to pay that much for you. But if you don't have mutual acceptance yet, who can know? When you look at the bottom line—the cash required for closing—it can appear that a particular loan officer is making things cheaper for you when they have absolutely no knowledge of whether or not that will happen.

Here's the exception: If you require the seller to pay a certain sum of your closing costs to make the purchase possible, then the loan officer can specify that as a requirement on both your GFE and on your preapproval letter.

The New Good Faith Estimate Designed by HUD

True to government standards, they replaced the simple one-page form with a convoluted three-page form. And instead of highlighting the important aspects that affect borrowers now, they highlighted two loan programs that are nearly as extinct as the dinosaur: the Option ARM and the balloon payment loan. (As a reminder, the Option ARM is the negative amortization loan where your balance goes up every month. The balloon loan requires you to refinance or pay off the entire loan balance after a certain number of years.)

On the new GFE proposed by the government agency, they added a "shopping cart." You've got to be kidding me, right? A shopping cart for a mortgage? Funny, I know, but the quaint little "cart" they have for borrowers to try to compare offers is laughable. They would have been better off just mandating the usage of the clear, one-page GFE mortgage brokers have been using all along.

Why the New GFE Fails Borrowers

By looking at what's wrong with the U.S. government's new GFE, you will be better equipped to get your best financing. So here goes...

Page 1, Important dates: There's a place for the loan officer to state how long the interest rate is good through. Every loan officer is rolling on the floor laughing about that because the rate could change literally one minute later. Rates change daily and throughout the day—with no advance notice. So when a loan officer writes "30 days" or any other time frame, you have to know it's meaningless until your rate is locked in. As for the other dates, they are also meaningless for the home shopper who does not yet have a signed purchase and sale agreement in hand.

Page 1, Summary of your loan: Loan amount, term (how many years the loan is for), interest rate, and payment are clearly listed here. Then, there are four questions to point out if you have a fixed rate, an adjustable rate, a balloon payment, or a prepayment penalty. All good on this section.

Page 1, Escrow account information: The property taxes and homeowner's insurance (hazard insurance) are lumped together here. On the old form, you could see how much the taxes were and how much the insurance was, which is clearer and better.

Page 1, Summary of your settlement charges: This is confusing for loan officers, so you know it was designed by government personnel; and I can just imagine how confusing it is for borrowers.

Box A "Adjusted Origination Charges": You have to flip to the top of page 2 to reference what it's talking about. But the travesty here—the big misleading sham—is that the current law says only mortgage brokers have to properly disclose the Yield Spread Premium here; and that banks and direct lenders can skip it, leave it blank, draw a line, put N/A, or whatever else to skirt the issue and keep you in the dark. And they're not calling it a YSP any more. It's referred to as "You receive a credit of $___ for this interest rate of ___%." What goes in the first blank is the YSP. Then, the instructions tell you to flip to the middle of page 3 and use the "trade-off table" to look at your options for "settlement charges" versus "interest rate." Confused? Me too, the first three times I read it. Finally, I figured out the way this form is set up, it assumes the "credit" or YSP will actually be credited back to you instead of paying the lender. But what about all the people who want their lender to be paid with the YSP or "credit" because they choose to pay zero percentage points up front? This form makes no sense for that scenario or all the times when it's a combination thereof. And I'm still fuming about the fact that brokers and not bankers have to fill in all the banks!

👎 Bad Practice

Calling the YSP or overage "a credit of $___ for this interest rate of ___%." This is confusing and misleading for the borrower.

👍 Good Practice

Clearly disclosing the premium that is paid by the wholesale lender to the mortgage broker a Yield Spread Premium (YSP).

Box B "Your Charges for All Other Settlement Services": Flip to page 2 again to see this is the nonlender, third-party costs, such as appraisal, title, recording, and so on. But then it also includes the costs that are not fees but part of a loan's settlement costs, such as the setup of escrow for your taxes and insurance and the number of days between funding and the end of the month.

The committee that designed the new three-page GFE claims it worked well with their test group. Mortgage brokers dispute the claim saying their test group did not represent an accurate cross section of borrowers. I'd like to know what *you* think. Send me an e-mail through my Web site, www.AskCarolynWarren.com.

Coming Up Next

It could be disastrous if the interest rates zoomed up by a percent or more while your loan was in progress. You'd be counting on a certain payment, and then find out you had to pay much more. That is what the interest rate lock is for—to prevent you from an unpleasant surprise like that. The next chapter explains how the lock works and how to know when to lock in.

18

When to Lock in Your Rate, When to Float

I've heard a lot of jokes about forecasting interest rates. Such as, when people ask you what rates are going to do, tell them to call the psychic hotline at 1-800-NOBODY-KNOWS. Or, tell them to wait just a minute while you consult your crystal ball.

If you don't like those strategies, then you can do what I do and look at the current market, recent interest rate history, and what indicators are coming up—in that order—then make the best decision you can. (Details about the indicators are discussed later in this chapter.) To avoid the uncertainty of a changing market, locking in your interest rate will give you peace of mind. Here's how it works…

To Avoid Being Victim of a Changing Market, Lock In

If you're counting on a certain interest rate and monthly payment, the last thing you need is to get to the closing and find they've gone way up. So to prevent that from happening, you can lock in your rate.

You tell your loan officer you want to lock in at 6 percent (or whatever the current rate is), he or she sends in a lock request to the lender's lock department, and you get a written rate lock confirmation. This guarantees you 6 percent, no matter what the market does. Rates could skyrocket to 8 percent in the next week and never come back down to 6 again, and you would still get your 6 percent rate because you locked in.

But what if you locked in at 6 percent and the rate went down to 5.75 percent? Can you get the lower rate? No, because it's locked, and that is a commitment. Asking to break the commitment is like asking your fiancée, "If I marry you and then a prettier girl comes along, can I switch to her?" You can't have it both ways. Either you get the security of a guaranteed rate, or you float and take your chances. That said, there are exceptions.

Float-Down Option

Some lenders will allow what's called a "float-down option." They allow you to make one change in your interest rate, even though it's locked—*if the rates are significantly lower.* Usually this ends up being a compromise between the original rate you locked in and the new lower rate, but it's a good option and everybody ends up happy.

Switching Lenders

Another option is that your mortgage broker might switch to a different wholesale lender if rates drop drastically. They're not supposed to do that very often because the first lender gets burned. They've put your loan on the books, put a good deal of work into it, and then get stiffed and make zero, which isn't fair. No decent broker would switch lenders for an eighth or quarter percent drop; but if rates dropped a whole percentage point, either the original lender would allow a compromise with a float-down option to keep the business, or your broker could switch lenders. If you have any questions about this, always consult with your current loan officer first and foremost. Don't commit the dastardly deed of snaking off to a different loan officer and leaving your hardworking professional in the lurch. Give him or her a chance to keep your business because loan officers don't get paid a salary, and they end up making zero for all the work they've done when the loan doesn't close.

Three Ways to Know When to Lock

When a client asks me when they should lock in their rate, I always make it clear that the final choice is theirs, but then to offer some assistance in making that important decision, I look at three things.

1. What is the current market?

If it's a declining market, there is little risk to waiting to lock in your rate. Rates will vary from day to day, but overall, they're going lower. I read the daily reports and make a decision based on that.

If it's a rising market, lock in as soon as you see a day with a pretty good rate. Even in a rising market, the graph showing daily interest rates is not a straight line up; there are zigzags, so catch one of the down zags and consider yourself fortunate.

If it's a volatile market, it's extremely difficult to predict what will happen next. As I'm writing, we are in a volatile market. The graph charting interest rates looks like a giant W. Rates go down and quickly up again and down and up. The problem is that you never know where the lowest point is, or how long it will last.

One morning I called my client and suggested she lock in because rates had come down from 6.25 to 5.75. She said she'd check with her husband and get back to me. Two hours later she called me back to say she was pretty sure they wanted to lock and her husband was going to call me. In the meantime, rates went from 5.75 to 6, and I had to give her the bad news. Soon, her husband called and expressed his disappointment in the higher rate, but said to go ahead and lock. As soon as I hung up, I went to lock in for them and saw the rates had risen again, from 6 to 6.25. I didn't have the heart to disappoint them for a second time in one morning, so I took the loss personally and locked them in at 6 flat. But that's an example of how rates can change rapidly in a volatile market.

If it's a volatile market and rates have dipped, lock in and don't worry if rates drop another eighth—you got a good deal. But if it's a volatile market and rates have just gone up by a half, I wouldn't lock in. Some people do; they think, oh my gosh, rates are going up, I'd better lock fast, and they lock at the top of the W. Personally, I would float and wait for it to come back down again. Admittedly, I have a higher tolerance for risk than some. If you can't sleep at night for worrying about interest rates, lock in and be done with it.

2. What is the recent history with interest rates?

This information can be helpful in determining where you might be in the graph on any given day. You can see what I mean by what happened to one of my recent homebuyers.

Rates had been fluctuating from 5.625 to 6.5. But most recently, 5.75 was the best I'd seen, and rates had been up in the 6s for the past several weeks. Then one day we got a dip to 5.75. There was a locking frenzy! All the loan officers I knew were calling their clients and locking in. I called one of my clients who was buying a home for $422,000 in Connecticut.

"Rates have dropped to 5.75. I highly recommend that you lock in because this rate might not last, and it's the lowest we've seen in weeks," I said.

After thinking about it, they said, "We want to hold off and see if rates drop to 5.5 percent."

The next day, rates went up to 5.875, and I suggested they might want to lock before it went even higher.

They decided to float to see if it would come down more.

The next day, rates went up to 6.

The next day, rates went up to 6.125.

The next day, rates went up to 6.25.

It was painful, like watching *Deal or No Deal* when the contestant keeps opening cases and the banker's offer keeps getting worse and worse.

The next day, rates went up to 6.375.

The next day, rates went up to 6.5.

The husband e-mailed me and said they were kicking themselves for not locking in at 5.75 when I suggested it.

Over the next two weeks, rates fluctuated in the 6s. Then mercifully, the rate dropped to 5.875 again shortly before it was time to draw the loan documents. They locked in and were able to sleep once again. If rates had stayed at 6.5, we would have been forced to take it because you have to lock your rate before the Loan Note and other documents can be printed. The lesson is that when the rate drops to the bottom of the big W, it's risky holding out for a new low in a volatile market.

3. Look at what indicators are coming up.

Mortgage rates are based on mortgage-backed securities or mortgage bonds.

Mortgage rates are not set by the president or the Federal Reserve Board. Some people don't understand that, so when they hear on the news there has been a federal rate cut, they think this means mortgage rates just went down. That's not so. Those cuts are to short-term rates and affect short-term loans such as credit cards and auto loans. By contrast, the 30-year mortgage is a long-term rate and might move in the opposite direction of the short-term rates.

Mortgage rates are primarily influenced by indicators such as (1) investors' perception of inflation, (2) confidence in the economy or lack thereof, and (3) the fluctuations of the stock market.

Think of it this way: Mortgage rates love bad news. That is, when the unemployment rate gets worse, when there is a decrease in durable goods orders, when a piece of economic data shows weakness, then mortgage rates go down.

That is, most of the time.

I subscribe to some daily reports that give me an idea as to whether locking or floating is recommended and pass on that information to my clients, as do many loan officers. To see the national overnight average for interest rates, go to BankRate.com; it's right on the home page. Don't fill in the blank for your zip code because that's a trap to take your application online (see Chapter 26, "Stop Clicking on Mortgage Ads"). Be aware that the average rates are for loans with up-front percentage points in an Origination Fee and/or Discount Fee, and for conventional loans, not the larger Jumbo Loans. Also, the figure is for yesterday's average; it is not up-to-the-minute.

Now for a frequently-asked question and then a warning.

How Long Is a Rate Lock?

You choose how long you want the lock period to be. The most common is 30 days. An extended lock for 45 days costs an additional fee of .125 percent, and a 60-day lock costs an additional fee of .25

percent. You can choose to add that percentage to the interest rate rather than pay the extra fee, if desired. Some lenders offer a 90-day lock. Unless you're in a rising rate market, you wouldn't choose to pay more to lock in for the longer time period. In fact, for saving money, you might choose a 15-day lock, when you're that close to closing.

Please note that to lock in your rate, you must have an address to tie it to, so you cannot lock in while you're still house hunting.

Warning: Get It in Writing

In mortgage land, verbal quotes and promises mean nothing. *Get it in writing* is the rule. After your rate is locked, you should receive a written Rate Lock Confirmation Letter within 24–48 hours. Keep this because it is your guarantee. If you get to the signing table and discover the interest rate is wrong, pull out this confirmation and refuse to sign until they correct it.

Back in the day of subprime lending, boosting up the rate a little at the end was a common practice. The poor homebuyers felt too intimidated to make much of a fuss, and they signed anyway—which sent a message to those sleazy sharks that they could get away with it. When I worked at Ameriquest and Green Tree/Conseco Financial, we loan officers would argue with our managers for lower rates because our managers were forever jacking up the interest rate on our loans to increase company profit. Why? Because they were under pressure from their regional managers, who were also under pressure from the executives above them. It was an ongoing battle.

One day one of my colleagues was in a loud argument with the manager of Green Tree Financial over the interest rate.

"I've already promised them this rate!" he shouted.

"Come on, don't tell me they're not going to sign just because the rate is a little higher. It only affects their payment by $70. You should have given them a higher rate in the first place because their debt ratio is so low. They can handle it," said the manager.

More arguing ensued, and I think the manager won. But the borrowers could have stopped the whole thing simply by standing up and threatening to walk out. There's no way the manager would have let a loan fall out. They'd do what they had to in order to keep a loan.

This is one of the reasons I am biased toward mortgage brokers. They don't have any kind of pressure from management to sell higher rates. A loan officer who is a mortgage broker has total and complete autonomy to price a loan any way he or she wants, as long as they're within the range offered on the rate sheet.

And if anything "funny" should happen with your interest rate, you've got your written Rate Lock Confirmation Letter to set it right.

👎 Bad Practice

Being a victim of bait-and-switch shenanigans.

👍 Good Practice

Getting a written Rate Lock Confirmation Letter and keeping it as your guarantee to receive the interest rate and up-front points (Origination Fee or Broker Fee, and Discount Fee) you were promised.

When Rates Spike Unexpectedly

I've seen homebuyers get upset to the point of tears over bad surprises with interest rates. And I'll admit I used to get stressed out myself. One evening I was worrying about the rate hike that had occurred earlier that day. I hated telling my clients rates were up. This particular day, I knew I was going to have to call a homebuyer the next morning to tell them rates—and, therefore, their monthly payment—was going to be higher. I knew they'd be upset, and this was making me upset. It had gotten to the point where I wasn't sleeping well at night.

In an effort to chill out before going to bed, I switched on the television. I happened to tune in to a program already in progress where some doctors were in conference about a patient's condition. The patient had something terminal and was going to die soon. One of the doctors got the task of breaking this news to the family who was sitting out in the waiting area, hoping for and expecting good news. Can you imagine being that doctor and having to walk down the long hall, look into the faces of the mother and father, and tell them that their son would soon die?

The TV doctor trudged down the hospital corridor looking like he had a three-ton weight on his back, and as gently as he could, he explained to the parents their son's condition. Was there any hope for a recovery? Unfortunately, no, and he was so sorry. The loving parents collapsed in a flood of tears. The scene was heartwrenching. And then a thought occurred to me: This constitutes a true tragedy.

Interest rates going up—that is hardly a tragedy! It put things into perspective for me, and it's a lesson I've never forgotten.

Coming Up Next

What does it take to get approved? What's the minimum down payment? How much money do you need in the bank? How can you get an exception to too-strict rules? All this and more coming up next.

19

What Does It Take to Get Approved?

Before we get in to the rules and regulations for loan approval, here's a peek at what goes on behind the scenes—an actual conversation that took place this week between a loan officer, the account executive for the wholesale lender, and the underwriter. And by the way, this is the stuff you'll never read about in books written by ghostwriters for "big names" because they've never worked behind closed doors themselves. They're as clueless as the public, if you don't mind my saying so.

Anyway, I'm the loan officer for a refinance and we're at the stage of final review and approval, just before going to draw the loan documents for signing. I get a call from the account executive at the wholesale lender.

"I need you to talk to my underwriter," he says. "She's having 'all kinds of issues' with this loan." (The borrower has a 780 credit score and there is a lot of equity in the property, so this is no borderline risky loan.)

One of the issues is that he has a house address and a different mailing address, which is a mailbox company for people who travel a lot. In this age of ID theft, he doesn't want his personal statements sitting in a mailbox on the street for weeks while he's traveling, so he rents a mailbox. This makes sense, and it's easily explained, especially because his job is of a traveling nature. But the underwriter is still suspicious about why he has two addresses. She does an online search and verifies that the mailing address is indeed a commercial address. Even still, she's not convinced there isn't something fishy or fraudulent going on.

The account executive says to me, "Just call her now and talk to her. Once she talks to you, she'll know you're an honest person. There are a lot of unscrupulous loan officers out there and she won't believe me either because there are a lot of unscrupulous account executives as well." (Remember, this is mid-2009 after the subprime sharks have all closed their doors.)

So I call and explain the situation, including the fact that I live in the same city, know the neighborhood, and so on. She says, "Okay, if you can get me an advertisement for the mailbox company, I'll accept it."

I drag out the two-ton Yellow Pages, find their ad, and we're good to go. Then, the account executive lets me in on another little secret. He says their underwriters are now held accountable for any bad loan they approve, and that's why they document the heck out of every teeny, tiny detail in the loan file.

On another loan, a refinance where two single people were applying together, the underwriters were suspicious as to whether the girlfriend actually lived there. Even though she provided a pay stub with the address on it and they had a joint bank account, the underwriters felt they couldn't be too careful about including her income. They asked for someone to go out to the house to check.

The loan officer made the mistake of telling them this, and they were furious.

"That's an invasion of our privacy! We will not open the door," they said. And they asked, "Can they do that?"

The answer is, yes they can, and they did. The lender holds the money; therefore, they can make up whatever requirements they deem necessary in order to validate the borrowers' ability to pay.

So one evening, an appraiser knocked on their door; and sure enough, they opened it, and the girlfriend was there. The loan got approved and funded. So you see, documentation beyond what's in the basic outline may be required. And yes, they can do that—and more.

Although Fannie Mae and Freddie Mac publish their guidelines for loan approval, individual lenders may add their own requirements. What's more, individual underwriters vary as to their interpretation of some of the rules. Some are more lenient and believe common sense plays a part in making a judgment call; whereas others are sticklers for the highest possible standard of the "letter of the law." And when it comes to sticky details, never underestimate the power of relationships. This is why you want to choose a loan officer who will be your personal advocate and who has a stellar reputation in the industry. If you have an unusual situation or are borderline for meeting the approval requirements, having a loan officer who knows how to present your loan application and write a strong letter of support can make all the difference. Now on to the rules for getting approved.

Following are general guidelines taken from a 50+-page document dated March 13, 2009.

Down Payment Requirements

Your down payment must be fully documented, and it must be your own money or gift money from family. It cannot be a side loan or an advance from a credit card. Your family cannot borrow money and give it to you for a down payment. The gift money must also be sourced and they have to show they had the ability to give by providing a bank statement with sufficient funds.

If you just came into a large sum of cash, which you'll use for your down payment, you need to document where it came from. For example, provide the paperwork showing it was an income tax return, from the sale of a vehicle, and so on. If you transfer money from one account to another, you'll need to provide statements from both bank accounts. A complete paper trail for the down payment must be in your loan file.

- Primary Residence: 5 percent to 10 percent (10 percent if in a county that is a declining market or if a condo) for a conventional loan. For an FHA loan, 3.5 percent down. For a VA loan, 0 down.
- For a conventional loan, the borrower must provide at least 5 percent down payment from his/her own money when the total down payment is less than 20 percent. The remainder may come from gift money from family, a fiancé, or domestic partner.

- For an FHA loan, the entire down payment may be gift money (but assets are required).
- Second Home: 20 percent.
- Investment/Rental: 25 percent. (No gift money allowed.)

Asset Requirements

You provide all the pages of your bank statement to show assets. Why not just the first page showing the balance? Because the underwriter looks to see if you wrote checks that bounced, had insufficient funds to cash. The underwriter also looks to see if there are any uncharacteristically large deposits, and if so, you must document where that money came from.

- For primary residence purchases, usually two months' total new payment required to be in reserves.
- For second homes, usually two months' total new payment required to be in reserves.
- For investment property purchases, six months' total new payment required to be in reserves.

Credit Score Requirements

Use the middle score of three or the lowest score of two. If two people are applying together, the credit of the person with the worst credit is used for qualifying and pricing.

- FICO score: 620+ with a 20 percent down payment conventional, or 3.5 percent down for FHA. Some lenders will allow a lower credit score on FHA loans when there is manual underwriting, meaning a human being makes a judgment call based on the overall picture of the application. Compensating factors like a high income, low debt ratio, large assets, and job stability might help to overcome a low credit score.
- FICO score: 680 with a down payment less than 20 percent.

- No credit score/low score: Requires the underwriter to make a judgment call based on what the credit report says, income, and other factors. Although a person with no credit score or a lower credit score can be approved, the cost of the loan will be significantly higher.

Adverse Credit

Having negative credit does not mean you can't get a mortgage, but the underwriter does want to see that you are back on track with your finances now.

- Outstanding judgments, collections, and charge-offs usually must be paid off; however, there are exceptions, such as when the Desktop Underwriting (DU) software approves the loan without demanding payoff and the derogatory account does not threaten the mortgage from recording in first position. (This is a shortened summary, not the entire rule.) For a married couple, the loan may be done in the name of the spouse with good credit only, if that person has the income to qualify on his or her own.
- Bankruptcy Chapter 7: Four years prior to the credit report date for conventional loans. Two years for FHA.
- Bankruptcy Chapter 13: Two years from discharge date or four years from dismissal date.
- Bankruptcy due to Extenuating Circumstances, Chapters 7 and 13: Two years from the discharge or dismissal date.
- Consumer Credit Counseling: Preferred to be out of CCC and have reestablished credit, but there are exceptions, such as when DU approves the loan without regard to the debt counseling program.

Income Requirements

For your income to count, it must be current income. Don't send your W2 from the high-paying job you had last year if you've been laid off, because it will go straight into the shredder. You don't receive that income anymore, so it doesn't help prove you have the ability to pay for the loan you're applying for. Similarly, future, projected income doesn't count either, because even the best of plans can go awry.

- Varies according to lender and the strength of the loan application; for example, a person who is making a large down payment can get approved with a higher debt-to-income ratio than a person with minimum down and minimum assets in reserves. But a general guideline is 43 percent to 45 percent debt-to-income ratio when using gross income and all obligations listed on the credit report. But I have seen 50 percent and even higher DTI ratios approved when the application was strong.
- Unearned income (disability, social security, spousal maintenance, child support) may be counted as long as it will continue for at least three more years.
- Must provide income documentation, such as two years' W2s, current pay stubs for one month pay, or an award letter for disability income.
- Self-employed: Minimum of two years' tax returns required to verify two years of self-employment. Use your Adjusted Gross Income and average the years together, or if income declined, go by the newer, lesser income. (The actual income calculation is more complex, but this is a good, general guideline.)
- Unemployment: Can be used only if it is a normal, ongoing part of your job, such as in construction work or commercial fishing.

Eligible Borrowers

Here are the guidelines for who is eligible to get a mortgage in the United States; other countries might have similar requirements, but check with your loan officer.

If you are an illegal alien who is using the social security number of a dead person, be aware that underwriters are trained to track down that information and you will be denied.

- U.S. citizens, permanent resident aliens, nonpermanent resident aliens. Foreign nationals are ineligible. Minimum age is 18.
- Nonoccupant coborrowers are eligible, but the people who will be living in the property must have the credit to qualify on their own. Having a cosigner does not overcome your low credit score.

Please note that underwriting guidelines change from time to time and vary between lenders, so this is for general educational purposes only.

Coming Up Next

Should you use a real estate agent or make a go of it on your own? Will you save money as a homebuyer if you go through the seller's agent? Do real estate agents make too much money for the work they do? These and other thought-provoking questions are answered in the next chapter.

20

Why You Need Agent Representation

"The real estate agent shall be absolutely honest, truthful, faithful, and efficient…"

—From the first article of code written in 1913 for real estate professionals

Do you, like a lot of people, have a sneaking suspicion that your real estate agent is making a killing, at your expense?

Could you possibly snap up a better deal by calling the agent on the sign rather than using your own buyer's agent?

What do you need to watch out for if you buy new construction from a builder?

Will you come out ahead by selling your own home?

This chapter answers these intriguing questions and more; but first, you should know that in every state, a license is required to mediate between buyer and seller for a fee, except in states where a lawyer can also perform that job.

Real estate agents are required to attend classes, pass exams, and continue their education by attending classes annually. If they are a member of the National Association of Realtors, they are held to a high standard—the 17 Articles of the Code of Ethics—which is strictly enforced.

17 Pledges That Are Required to Be a Realtor

1. Pledge to put the interest of buyers and sellers ahead of their own, and to treat all parties honestly. Shall not deliberately mislead property owners as to market value. Shall not mislead buyers as to savings or other benefits. Shall submit offers and counteroffers objectively and as quickly as possible. Shall preserve confidential information.

2. Shall not exaggerate, misrepresent, or conceal pertinent facts. And is obligated to investigate and disclose when situations warrant.

3. Shall cooperate with other brokers when it is in the best interests of their client to do so. Shall disclose the existence of accepted offers.

4. Shall disclose if they represent family members who own or are about to buy real estate, or if they themselves are a principal in a real estate transaction, that they are licensed to sell real estate.

5. Shall not provide professional services in a transaction where the agent has a present or contemplated interest without disclosing that interest.

6. Shall not collect any commissions without the seller's knowledge nor accept fees from a third party without the seller's express consent.

7. Shall not accept fees from more than one party without all parties' informed consent.

8. Shall not comingle client funds with their own.

9. Shall attempt to ensure that all written documents are easy to understand and will give everybody a copy of what they sign.

10. Shall not discriminate in any fashion for any reason on the basis of race, color, religion, sex, handicap, familial status, or national origin.

11. Shall be competent, conforming to standards of practice, and shall refuse to provide services for which they are unqualified.

12. Shall be honest and truthful in communications, advertising, and marketing.

13. Shall not practice law unless they are a lawyer.

14. Shall cooperate if charges are brought against them and present all evidence requested.

15. Shall not make false or misleading statements about their competition. Agree not to file unfounded ethics complaints.

16. Shall not solicit another Realtor's client nor interfere in a contractual relationship.

17. Shall submit to arbitration to settle matters and not seek legal remedies in the judicial system.

For Homebuyers

If you were facing a grisly opponent in a court of law and hundreds of thousands of dollars were at stake, would you (a) ask your opponent if you could share his or her attorney, or (b) get your own legal representation so you had an attorney on your side, watching out for your own best interests, navigating the legal waters for you?

Clearly, there's only one reasonable answer: You would insist on having your own attorney, your own expert, to stick up for you. The same principle applies in buying real estate. You need your own agent representation.

Don't Call the Agent on the Sign!

If you call the seller's agent, the one listed on the For Sale sign, it's like calling your opponent's attorney. You could easily give out information about yourself, your financing, your price range, and so on that the seller's agent shouldn't know. Typically, the conversation goes something like this…

You ask, "What is the price of the home listed at this address?"

The agent responds, "That's a great-looking house, isn't it? You should see the inside; the kitchen has been completely remodeled, it's truly gourmet, and it has the most gorgeous granite countertops—by the way, what is your name?"

You get caught up in the excitement, in the agent's enthusiasm, and you say, "My name is Carolyn Warren."

"So nice to talk with you, Carolyn, and what price range are you looking in?"

"We're looking at homes in the $425,000 to $450,000 range." Oops! There you've just given out your top dollar. What if this house is listed at $449,500 and your buyer's agent advises you that it's on the high side and should go for $430,000 tops? You've just shot yourself in the wallet by revealing that you could pay more. Your own agent can just as easily tell you the asking price, so conduct all your communication through your agent.

But even more important, by law, the seller's agent is required to get the highest price and all the best terms for his client, the seller.

Get a Load of This!

Some naive homebuyers think they'll get a better price if they use the seller's agent, but that is rarely the case. I had a client, a married couple, who was buying a $629,000 home in Southern California, and they decided to call the agent on the sign, hoping he'd give them a cheaper price because he'd be making double commission.

When the deal was complete, I asked the agent, "Does a homebuyer get a better deal when they use the listing agent as their agent too?"

He chuckled with amusement and then answered, "Well… not really, that's mostly a marketing tactic." Interesting response from an agent who just had that opportunity!

But to be sure, I sought out the opinion of real estate agents all across the country. Responses came from all four corners of the United States with a near-unanimous response: "No, you don't get a lower price by using the seller's listing agent."

Why Using the Seller's Agent Is a *Bad* Idea

"A dual agent is a disloyal agent to both buyer and seller, and is mainly loyal to himself (or herself). If you agree to dual agency, you are then *on your own* to negotiate price and terms, and it's up to you to discover what is wrong with that property. Informed home buyers avoid dual agency."

—Gary Herbst, Buyers Edge Realty, Tarrytown, NY
www.BuyersEdgeRealty.com

Saving Homebuyers Money

"I have structured offers so my buyer clients' offers get accepted even when they are not the highest offer in multiple-offer situations. I have saved buyer clients money—as much as $25,000 less than they were prepared to spend—by presenting an offer with a letter to introduce my clients to the seller."

—Judy Moses, Pathway Home Realty Group Inc., MA, RI
www.PathwayHome.com

12 Reasons to Have a Buyer's Agent on Your Side

Now look at the following list and you'll see why I'm in favor of having your own real estate agent represent you.

1. A buyer's agent will do his or her best to ascertain the seller's hot buttons and position your offer accordingly. For example, will your ability to close quickly be advantageous to the seller who might be transferring jobs soon? Wendy Smith, a Realtor at Coldwell Banker Danforth in Seattle, told me an interesting story. Her clients were a young couple who had only $500 for earnest money. Their offer was below the asking price. And then to complicate the situation, there was a competing offer coming in on the same house. Wendy Smith did some digging and learned the sellers were in a hurry to move. Using this information, she wrote a cover letter highlighting the fact that

her clients could close in just two weeks—and their offer was accepted!

2. A good buyer's agent will listen to your criteria and save you time by searching out homes that might be a good match. Sometimes, a buyer's agent has to listen "between the lines" to figure out how your desires can match *what you can afford*. Here's a real life example of that...

A couple moving from the rural town of Spokane, Washington, to Seattle specified that they wanted a one-level ranch style home on at least half an acre—and their top price was $270,000. The Realtor didn't insult them by rolling her eyes, but $270,000 doesn't buy a half acre of anything in the city. So instead, she showed them homes she thought would fit their family. As it turned out, they fell in love with a tri-level style in an upscale neighborhood on a quarter-acre lot. She did a good job of interpreting their needs and finding a home they could afford—and in the process, saved them many miles of driving and many hours of searching in frustration.

A buyer's agent might even be able to show you a property that hasn't been listed yet, thereby eliminating competitive bids. They have access to information the public does not have.

👎 Bad Practice

Getting locked in to one narrow set of criteria at a set price point.

👍 Good Practice

Communicating with your agent what is most important to you and keeping an open mind. If a home doesn't appeal to you, let your agent know why so she can help refine your search.

3. An expert buyer's agent will do a market analysis so you know how much lower you could *reasonably* offer. For example, could you make a lowball offer of 15 percent off the price, or would that cause the seller to turn you down flat?

4. A buyer's agent knows the trends of local home prices, including if and how much they might be trending downward. Something like that could be used to your advantage in making an offer below asking price.

Secret Information Sources

"Professionals study their real estate market daily. Professionals have access to many sources of useful and accurate information that the public isn't aware of or can't access. Recently, I found some clients a home that was exactly what they wanted, and it was not even listed yet."

—Heath Coker, Cape Group Real Estate, Cape Cod
www.CapeGroup.com

5. A buyer's agent knows how much you are likely to get in a seller contribution toward your closing costs. For example, just recently a buyer's agent told me in her area, sellers were readily accepting offers asking for the seller to contribute 3 percent toward their closing costs. How helpful to have that knowledge, as opposed to picking a number out of the blue, or not asking for any money for closing costs at all! That tip alone could save you thousands of dollars in closing costs. Many homebuyers negotiating on their own don't think of or don't have the courage to ask the seller to contribute $5,000 or more to their closing costs; but real estate agents commonly do—particularly in a buyer's market.

6. Your agent keeps your personal information confidential, per law. You can (and should) let your agent know how much you are approved for and how much higher you could go—your agent is your trusted advisor.

   For instance, if you've been approved for $300,000 but want to offer $280,000; for obvious reasons, you don't want the seller's agent to know you've got an extra 20 grand available.

7. A buyer's agent has access to the cumulative number of days the property has been on the market, so you can strategize your purchase offer accordingly.

"We Got a Great Deal"—NOT!

"Without an agent, most individuals don't negotiate as much as they should. What a buyer's agent is going to do is pull up comps on what the property sold for, use other less-expensive comparables to negotiate the price down, and pull up tax information to see what is owed on the property and how financially sound or motivated the seller is. The buyer's agent's role is to stay out of the emotional aspect and negotiate as low as possible. Typically, an individual will get too emotionally attached.

"I had a good friend who bought a property through the selling agent who was kicking in and reducing some of his commission. They thought they got a great deal. But they ended up paying about $35,000 more than when it was listed a month prior. I have since come across the selling agent, and they feel like they got very lucky the buyer didn't have an agent to pull up history on the property."

—Daniel Merrion, City Point Realty, Chicago
     www.CityPointRealty.com

8. A buyer's agent looks out for important terms in the agreement that you might not think of so that you don't jeopardize your earnest money. You'll want a clause about approving the inspection report and a financing contingency—both of which are time sensitive. Your agent can spell out furnishings the seller might be willing to leave with the house such as appliances and window coverings. The date of occupancy is another hot topic that buyers often overlook. Without your agent, you might not notice a phrase that says "closing plus three days." The seller specifies closing on a Friday but with that phrase, you might not move in until the following Monday. That surprise has hit a lot of folks unaware.

9. A buyer's agent looks for the disclosure of material facts. Items such as a roof that leaks or an interior sump pump could affect desirability and price, for instance.

10. A buyer's agent can recommend a qualified, objective home inspector and pest inspector who will give you a thorough report. This in itself can save you thousands of dollars and even prevent disaster.

11. A buyer's agent handles the uncomfortable bargaining, going back and forth on price, and other important details. He or she acts as a buffer, protecting you from gasps, shouts, insults, curses, threats, and attempts at intimidation. You might be surprised at what goes on behind the scenes. It's not unusual for agents to play head games. On one transaction, the seller's agent took on an angry posture as she said to the buyer's agent, "Okay, we'll take your offer, BUT you better not ask for ANYTHING on the inspection." It was a bold attempt at intimidation—one that most buyers would have fallen victim to—but it didn't slow down the buyer's agent one iota from presenting a list of items to be repaired, per the inspection report. And guess what? The sellers gave in. How great is it to sit comfortably at home while your agent does the dirty work for you! Even if you're the bold, confrontational type, getting into a war of words and wit with the seller is unwise when you're the buyer. Let your agent be the "bad guy" in negotiating.

12. A buyer's agent is free of charge to you! This wraps it up: There is not one single advantage of going without your own professional, expert representation. Therefore, you definitely want your own licensed real estate agent to represent you.

What If It's "For Sale By Owner"?

It is my opinion, based on years of observation from being in the mortgage business, that you do not come out ahead by negotiating with a FSBO (For Sale By Owner) property on your own.

First, homeowners who decide to take on the inconvenience and risk of having strangers tramp through their house—without a licensed, professional agent present—are not doing so because they intend to give you a steal of a deal. Typically, people selling themselves are penny-pinchers who are looking to pocket more. It is their perception that a licensed, trained professional is not worth his or her commission because they don't understand the totality of what is behind a real estate transaction. So please, don't expect "a deal" by getting a FSBO. Most of those properties are overpriced from the get-go.

Second, if your one and only dream home does happen to be a FSBO, you can still have your buyer's agent present your offer and handle the legal documents. In that case, your agent may be paid by either the seller or you, depending on how it is negotiated; but my opinion is that you will come out ahead using your agent's expert help, even if you pay their commission in this instance.

I have to tell you the most outrageous real estate transaction I ever witnessed involved a home that sat on acreage in northern Washington State. I was doing the loan for the buyers, and it happened that both the sellers and buyers met in the conference room of my office for the signing of an addendum to the Purchase Agreement.

Their purchase contract was a brief two-page form purchased at an office supply store rather than the long form used by real estate professionals. The buyers had handwritten a list of things they wanted to be left with the property that wasn't in the original agreement, but which had been discussed and agreed upon originally. Now they were meeting with the sellers to put it in writing.

Lord knows why they picked my office as the meeting grounds— or should I say battlegrounds? Anyway, the problem was, the sellers didn't remember it the way that the buyers did.

The sellers said, "We are not throwing in the window coverings, appliances, and those other things for free."

The buyers said, "Yes, you are! You already promised! We had a verbal agreement."

The sellers said, "We made no such promise and had no such agreement."

An argument ensued. Then, the argument escalated.

One party called the other "a liar." The wives tugged on their husbands' arms to calm down.

Just then, the seller popped up and loudly invited the buyer to "step outside to settle it." There I was sitting in the middle of this muddle and I couldn't believe how many articles of the Code of Ethics for Realtors were being violated. And now, on top of that, it was coming to blows!

If there hadn't been a long hallway and an elevator to go down, I think the two would have dashed out on the sidewalk for an immediate boxing match. I suggested that everyone take a breather and come back later to finish signing the addendum. The sellers stormed out of the room to cool down.

Eventually, they compromised on what would be left with the home.

Later, the buyers told me privately they were thrilled to be getting so much home on so much acreage at such a good price. They then clued me in to the fact that the home had appraised for $100,000 more just recently, and they were getting a steal of a deal.

"How do you know it appraised for that much more?" I asked.

"Because the sellers told us what they paid for it before," they said, eyes gleaming.

But it wasn't true. The previous purchase file was in our office, and the sellers were lying. The buyers weren't getting "a deal" at all.

And then two weeks later, I received a call from the buyers who were now disgruntled and disillusioned. They complained that the sellers—the very people who seemed so nice and cooperative at the beginning—left all kinds of "extra things" behind. Things like scrap metal, lumber, old tires, and piles of garbage bags on the land for them to clean up. They hadn't hauled the debris away as per their verbal agreement, and the new owners wanted to know if they had any recourse.

If only they had proper agent representation, they would have saved themselves so much angst and a lot of money, too.

Go back and read the 17 pledges a Realtor makes again. After you realize no one in a FSBO transaction is being held to that code, ask yourself if that's a situation you want to get involved in.

Warning for People Buying a New Construction Home

You see a street of gorgeous new homes going up. Maybe you even get there in time to pick out your own colors. How exciting! But whatever you do, don't make the colossal mistake of neglecting to have your own, independent buyer's agent.

Don't waltz into the builder's selling office and use the builder's agent. And whatever you do, don't preview or take a tour of the house without your buyer's agent being present, right from the very first look. The reason is that most, if not all, builders require that the buyer's agent accompany the buyer to the initial visit for the builder to cooperate with and compensate the buyer's agent.

Again, without having your own real estate agent representation, you are walking into a dual agent situation, and it's like using your opponent's attorney to give you advice. I don't care if they're the nicest people on Earth and are happy to help you; use your own buyer's agent who is not associated in any way with the builder-seller.

Time and time again, I've seen buyers of new homes get royally ripped off because they went with the agent who was set up in the office at the property.

A good buyer's agent representing you to the builder's selling agent will look out for your best interests in important legalities such as the following:

- Cancelation rights
- Too-good-to-be-true promotions
- Builder so-called "throw-ins" and credits (that you end up paying for)

You need that protection, and you certainly won't get it without professional representation.

A Grandiose Mess

"I believe that the agents and real estate brokers out there who are routinely practicing as dual agents (for both seller and buyer) are in it for the higher commission and don't care one bit about what is in the best interest of the buyer.

"As a listing agent, the right thing to do when a buyer approaches you to write the offer is to suggest that the buyer go and find their own buyer's agent to write it.

"Some listing agents will agree to take less of a commission from the seller if the listing agent is going to take both sides of the commission. It all sounds so nice that the seller saves money, the listing agent earns more in commissions by taking both sides of it, and the buyer may save a few dollars. Even if it were possible for the listing agent to represent both sides in a neutral fashion, there always exists the question as how the listing agent would handle a major dispute between the buyer and seller.

"Since the listing agent stands right in the middle between them, that would end up being some feat on the listing agent's part! Can you imagine trying to serve two masters when they're at odds over incomplete work, repairs, incomplete disclosures, etc.?

"As wonderful as it sounds for buyers to use the listing agent to write the offer for them and for sellers to agree to the dual agency, it has the ability to result in a real mess for both parties (and the agent). It's much better to avoid it from the very beginning and ensure that both buyer and seller have their own representation."

—Jamie Flournoy, San Jose, CA, Assist-2-Sell
www.SellingSanJoseHomes.com

For Home Sellers

Because home sellers are the ones who pay the real estate commissions, they're the ones who wonder if they're overpaying. Many people suspect agents make a killing. They think they're raking in the dough, pocketing more money than a Ph.D. or M.D. But is that really true?

Are You Paying Your Real Estate Agent Too Much?

The median annual salary for *full-time* real estate agents in 2007 was $40,600, according to the United States Bureau of Labor Statistics (www.bls.gov).[1] And in 2008, it decreased to $36,700. Clearly, they're not making a surgeon's income on part-time hours like so many people suspect. Frankly, it takes a tremendous amount of work to make a go of it. Only the top ten percent of full-time agents had a median annual salary of $106,790—and you can bet they have years of experience and have invested a significant amount of money into marketing themselves to get to that level.

Let's say you sell your house for $200,000. It would be typical for 3 percent to go to the listing agent. But wait, she probably has to split that with her employer, so instead of getting $6,000, she might get $3,000–$5,400. And that is before deducting the cost of the sign, newspaper ads, postcard mailings, open houses, and other marketing efforts. Furthermore, it might have taken months to earn that commission. When you break it all down, and calculate how long they work to close a transaction, the hourly wage does not come close to "making a killing."

And because your listing agent likely got you a higher price, better terms, and saved your heart, stomach, and blood vessels from a lot of unhealthy stress, it's reasonable to think you got a fair deal—no, make that a great deal.

When Does the Service Outweigh the Fee?

"Consumers often don't see behind the curtain. To them, all people who sell real estate look the same. However, when a problem arises, that is when the true pros distinguish themselves. And, at those times, we are saving them significantly more than the fee we earn.

"Sometimes it is because we keep the transaction moving forward. We know how to problem solve. We think of problems as puzzles and keep asking questions and digging until we find a remedy. Sometimes it is our negotiating skills, including offer preparation and presentation. I have earned sellers more money by continuing to engage the buyer's agent in negotiation, step by step.

"I work hard to improve my skills, investing in myself, networking and learning from the best, continuing to educate myself. And, in the end, my service to my clients far outweighs my fee."

—Judy Moses, Pathway Home Realty Group, Inc., MA, RI
www.PathwayHome.com

What About Selling Your House Yourself?

Are you the type of person who is a do-it-yourselfer? You mow your lawn, change your oil, prepare your taxes, and you even fix your clogged pipes and leaky faucets. But selling a piece of real estate that is worth hundreds of thousands of dollars is taking do-it-yourself to a whole new level.

First, do you feel safe letting in strangers when you're there alone? Do you want to risk becoming the victim of armed robbery, assault, or rape?

Even if you put "by appointment only" on your sign, people have the gall to ring your doorbell asking for "a quick look." Or they'll sit in front of your house and call on their cell for an immediate appointment. They figure you're anxious to sell, and they're the exception.

But let's say you live in a safe area and you're an ex-Marine, so safety is not a concern. Are you fully prepared to handle all the legalities—in our litigious society?

Sage Advice for Home Sellers

"Most homeowners have never seen a rescission, a hazard seller disclosure form, or an inspection response. Today we have material facts and environmental concerns that need to be addressed; and if it can be shown that there was anything the seller was aware of that wasn't disclosed in the proper way, it can leave them open for lawsuit—for years to come. Also, is the seller aware of the correct amount of earnest money that should be collected? On a contingency offer, is the time line short enough that they're not strung out too long by a would-be buyer, only to find they've wasted months? Home sellers need a full-service, full-time agent to protect them and keep them on the right track."

—Sam DeBord, RE/MAX, Seattle
www.SeattleHome.com

Let's say you live in a safe area, are an ex-Marine, and your spouse is an attorney who can handle the legal documents. Are you prepared to do the marketing? You can have the most appealing house in your county; and yet, it can languish away, unsold for months on end, if it isn't aggressively marketed. In grandma's day, you posted a sign in the yard and placed an ad in the newspaper, but it doesn't work that way in today's market. We live in the age of the Internet and in the age of networking. Although anyone can pop up a Web site, how many people are going to find it—*realistically?* How powerful is your network database of potential buyers? How extensive is your network of relationships in the real estate community? How good are your copywriting (sales writing) skills and your knowledge of how to showcase your home?

Never Underestimate the Power of Network Relationships

"I create open house fliers and then drive around the city to hand-deliver them to my colleagues in other real estate offices. When I chat up a particular property, it generates a lot of interest and excitement. My broker's open house events are an effective marketing tool for selling a home."

 —Wendy Smith, Coldwell Banker Danforth, Seattle, WA
  www.ColdwellBankerDanforth.com

The Power of a Strong Internet Presence

"The Internet has opened up marketing to the world. Now someone in Italy at a coffee shop can 'drive down your street' via the computer, so you had better have your 'Internet For Sale Sign' up. Real estate agents can provide a great marketing system to get your home in front of buyers. Some of those buyers are working with other real estate agents."

 —Don Williams, Prudential Georgia Realty, Gainesville, GA
  www.DonWilliams1.com

"A strong Internet presence is necessary for effective marketing. The Internet has changed the way buyers find real estate. The majority of people looking for real estate, especially in a vacation area like Cape Cod, use the Internet to find property. The average Internet user looks for property almost 250 miles from their current home."

 —Heath Coker, Cape Group Real Estate, Cape Cod, MA
  www.CapeGroup.com

"Real estate agents/brokers have advertising and marketing volume that home owners cannot compete with. For instance, our company website last year had over 1,125,000 visitors *and* our listings are featured on other websites as well through exclusive international websites.

"Real estate agents have a large referral base. We work with other agents as co-brokers who bring their buyers to a property.

"In 2008, only 15 percent of home owners sold their own homes. While saving commission may sound attractive, sellers cannot afford those odds."

—Ross Ellis, Halstead Property, LLC, NY, NY
www.Halstead.com

Last, but also of top importance, is price. If your home is priced too high, it will sit like a wallflower at a high school dance. On the other hand, if you price it too low, you lose money. Homeowners make their best "educated guess" about price, but real estate professionals who have their finger on the daily pulse of the market use comprehensive methods to arrive at an accurate selling price.

House Prices Differ from Micromarket to Micromarket

"Our team creates a sophisticated Forecasted Market Analysis for clients. This forward-thinking method prices the home ahead of the market and is more accurate than the traditional Comparable Market Analysis.

"We determine the home's value by calculating what a buyer is willing to pay based on absorption rates in the area, current inventory, the 12-month median price adjustment index, and probable buyer concessions that are current built in to over 98 percent of all offers in this market."

—Patrick Flynn, Keller Williams Broker and Certified Real Estate Instructor for the Seattle Realty Group, Seattle, WA
www.SeattleRealtyGroupLLC.com

How to Find a Real Estate Star

In some neighborhoods, you can't step outside and throw a rock without hitting a real estate agent's sign. Agents abound, but how do you locate not just a mediocre agent, but an exceptionally good one, a bona fide real estate star? For a free tip sheet containing valuable information, send me an e-mail through my Web site, www.AskCarolynWarren.com.

Coming Up Next

The next three chapters are for homeowners who are refinancing, so if you are a homebuyer, feel free to skip ahead to Chapter 24, "Unique Loans, Unique Situations."

Endnotes

1. http://www.bls.gov/oes/current/oes419022.htm, January 27, 2009.

21

Ten Things You Must Know Before You Refinance

Just for fun, see how you do on these ten True or False questions. Or, if you dislike quizzes, skip ahead and read through the answers, where you'll find important information every homeowner needs to know before refinancing.

Test Your Refinance I.Q.

T F **1.** When you refinance, you are starting over with a new loan.

T F **2.** In deciding whether or not to refinance, make your decision based on how much money you will be saving each month.

T F **3.** Consolidating all non-tax-deductible debt (auto loan, credit cards) by refinancing them into your mortgage is a good financial strategy.

T F **4.** When refinancing to lower your rate and payments, it's best to pay zero points (zero Origination Fee, zero Broker Fee, zero Discount Fee).

T F **5.** Taking $30,000 cash out in a refinance for home improvements instantly increases your home's value by $30,000, once the improvements are complete.

T F **6.** Refinancing every couple of years makes sense as long as you are lowering your interest rate each time.

T F **7.** As long as you get a quote for the interest rate and payment, you don't need to get a formal Good Faith Estimate when refinancing.

T F   **8.** If you refinance within a year of purchasing your home, most likely you will not need a whole new appraisal.

T F   **9.** If you have been paying on your mortgage for ten years or more, you should not refinance, because you'll be going backward.

T F **10.** When refinancing, you have to pay several months of taxes and insurance up front for setting up a new escrow account again, even though you already did that when you purchased the home.

Answers with Explanation

1. True. When you refinance, you are starting fresh with a brand-new loan. Consequently, you go through the process again, just as you did when you purchased the property. The difference is that in a refinance, you can roll the closing costs into the loan itself, rather than bring in cash for the closing costs.

The exception would be an FHA streamline refinance, where your current lender lowers the interest rate without having you go through the entire process again.

2. False. Don't make the decision on whether to refinance based *solely* on how much money you'll be saving each month. Although it is an important consideration, don't make your decision based on that alone. More details about this in the next chapter.

3. This is false; we cannot say categorically that rolling all your non-tax-deductible debt into your mortgage is a good strategy, even though many loan officers advise you to do so.

My first job in the mortgage business was with Long Beach Mortgage, and our manager instructed us to sweep the credit report for every open account and then to roll everything with a balance—no matter how small—into the refinance. "Always get the biggest loan you can," she said. This was to help us meet our monthly quota set by the corporate office and to increase profits. But there was another, more sinister, reason for rolling all debts into the refinance, and that was to show more "savings" by comparing their current monthly outgo with their new, proposed monthly outgo. Let's say you'll save only $40/month by refinancing your mortgage. That doesn't look like such a good deal. But if the loan officer also pays off your auto loan and four credit cards, he might be able to show you monthly savings of $250 in your total outgo. This is because you're stretching short-term loans into 30-year loans. By looking only at how much less you'll pay out per month, the refinance appears a lot more attractive than it actually is when you examine all aspects.

If you have a debt you'll pay off in less than two years, don't roll it into your 30-year loan. If you can easily manage the payments on your auto, why pay more by stretching it out longer? The time it would make sense is if you have four years to go on your car loan, but you will sell your house in three years. Now you're shortening your car loan and getting a tax deduction on the interest.

👎 Bad Practice

Rolling all of your debt into your new mortgage when you refinance. It costs more for a debt-consolidation refinance if your loan-to-value ratio is above 60 percent.

👍 Good Practice

Preserving as much equity as you can by managing short-term debt outside your mortgage. A no-cash out refinance is cheaper if your new loan puts your loan-to-value ratio higher than 60 percent.

4. False. When refinancing, paying zero points will not get you the lowest rate and payment. If rates are low, it makes sense to secure the lowest rate and payment by paying an Origination Fee. Why go halfway there, taking a compromise with the zero-point loan? It's one of those marketing come-ons you don't want to fall prey to. Compare zero points with paying a point to make your best decision. If you plan to keep your property long-term, you'll surely come out ahead by taking par rate—or even buying down the rate below par.

5. False. Making home improvements will not necessarily increase your home's value by the amount it costs. Too many people use the reasoning as an excuse to spend money they don't have. Instead of saving until they can pay cash for the new windows or updated kitchen, they go deeper into debt by taking cash out of their home equity. It comes down to impatience and an unwillingness to budget and save. Although it's true that kitchen and bathroom remodels increase a home's value, you aren't going to get an instant dollar-for-dollar equity boost. So often, I hear homeowners say, "My home is worth $25,000 more now because we replaced the old windows; painted inside and out; and replaced out the old, stained carpet with hardwood floors." But appraisers tell us that is not so. When you update your home, it is considered normal maintenance. The comparable homes used by an appraiser to determine value will most likely also have updated windows, floors, and paint.

6. False. Refinancing every couple of years does not make sense—*for you*. But it makes great sense for the loan officer who works on commission and wants to make money off his same customers every year or two. I'll never forget the tall, beautiful blonde from Norway—a "high producer" who enlightened me about her phenomenal success.

   She said, "I set up my customers to refinance every two years." Believe me, that was all about her income, not the homeowners' benefit. The problem with being a serial refinancer is that you never get ahead in the all-important goal of owning your home free and clear. Remember, the way mortgage payments are set up, the majority of your payments go to interest the first few years, so if you repeat years one to three over and over again, you never get past the point where you're putting a bigger chunk of your money toward your principal balance. Ideally, you don't want to refinance more than once; but be prepared to hear a lot of loan officers disagree with that.

👎 Bad Practice

Refinancing with no points every year or two to get the new, lower rate.

> **👍 Good Practice**
>
> Paying one point (or more when it makes sense) to get the lowest rate when you refinance—just once. That way, you make progress in paying off your mortgage.

7. A great big False! Federal law does require all loan officers, at all types of lending institutions, to provide you with a written Good Faith Estimate within three business days of taking an application. You have the right and the responsibility to review the costs and terms of your loan—and you need to do so right up front, before paying any money.

8. False. You will need a new appraisal report when you refinance, even if you purchased the property recently. In a market of rapidly changing values, an appraisal that is past 120 days old and/or ordered by another company will be considered out of date.

9. False again. There is a way you can refinance into a lower rate and still come out ahead in your amortization schedule (the chart that shows how much of your payment goes toward interest and how much toward principal balance). Simply take a 20-year loan or a 15-year loan. Compare rates and payments to make the best choice. Sometimes, the 20-year loan does not offer a better rate than the 30-year loan; but the 15-year loan does. If you are ten years into your mortgage, and you refinance into a lower rate and a 15-year loan, not only do you cut your interest, you also shave off five years of payments. Multiply your monthly principal and interest payment to see how much money that is! In the big picture, a 15-year loan saves tens of thousands of dollars, which is why it is my personal favorite loan product and the one I chose for myself. If you can afford it, take advantage of the colossal savings. Some loan officers say, "Take the 30-year loan and pay it off early; that way, you can have the lower payment if needed." In theory, that's good; but the vast majority of people stick to paying extra on their mortgage like they stick to a diet—and you know how that turns out.

👎 Bad Practice

Failing to consider the cost of starting over again with 30 years of payments when you refinance. If you are ten years into your loan, that is a significant step backward.

👍 Good Practice

Lowering your rate and shortening the term of your loan in one fell swoop. That makes for a double-whammy savings for you. If you can afford it, it's a great strategy.

10. True. When refinancing, you have to pay several months of taxes and insurance up front for setting up a new escrow account again, even though you already did that when you purchased the home. Now we've come full circle. The first question said refinancing is starting all over again with a new loan. That was the only other true statement in this quiz. Part of a new loan—whether it's a purchase loan or a refinance—is setting up the escrow account. But don't freak out—because you are not paying more. You are not being overcharged, and you are not being ripped-off. When the refinance funds and pays off your current mortgage, your current lender will refund to you every penny that is in your escrow account. This is because it is your money, set aside for taxes and insurance. You will automatically receive a check in the mail about two to three weeks after funding. So it ends up being "a wash." You don't pay more in taxes or insurance when you refinance. If you don't like the idea of adding the escrow set up into your new loan, then lower the loan amount of your refinance and bring in cash to close. You'll be getting money back shortly anyway, so why not?

How Did You Do?

If you got all ten answers right, then congratulations—you are summa cum laude. If you got eight to nine right, you did pretty well.

If you missed seven or more, it means you don't have experience in the mortgage business, and good for you for taking the initiative to read this information. If you have questions or comments about the quiz, I'd love to hear what you have to say. Please send me an e-mail via my Web site, www.AskCarolynWarren.com, where it says "Ask Carolyn."

Coming Up Next

Now on to the biggest question you'll have to answer if you're a homeowner: "Is it in my best financial interest to refinance?" If you are a homeowner, this chapter alone is worth getting the book for because it could save you thousands of dollars or prevent you from making a regrettable mistake.

22

Is Refinancing a Good Financial Move?

To determine whether refinancing is a good financial move, you have to look at all sides of the equation, not just the monthly savings.

Six Questions to Ask When Considering a Refinance

1. How much will you be saving every month with the new loan, compared with your current loan?
2. What is the cost of refinancing?
3. How many years are left on your loan now, and what is the term of your new loan?
4. How long do you plan to keep the property?
5. Are you getting out of a risky adjustable rate mortgage and into a secure fixed rate?
6. Will this refinance enable you to drop PMI (the monthly private mortgage insurance fee)?

As you can see, more than the monthly savings is at stake. Working as a loan officer, I've advised homeowners not to refinance, even though it meant forgoing a commission. Later, working as an account executive for a wholesale lender and working as a mobile notary signer, I observed millions of dollars in refinance loans speeding through to closing that never should have been done in the first place.

Some refinances are expensive loans with three to four points and high junk fees rolled into the loan. This was common during the days of subprime lending, but it still happens now. And the sad thing is that statistics show that most of the people who took these ultraexpensive loans refinanced again within two years—long before they recouped the cost with their monthly savings. Some paid three percentage points just to save $50 per month, due to fast-talking loan officers who were under unbelievable pressure from management to bring in loans. If they didn't meet a certain quota, they'd get written up and then fired. And each month, the corporate office increased the quota that had to be met. The loan officers were victims of corporate greed, just as the homeowners were.

A young male loan officer felt like he had no choice but to camp out on one homeowner's front porch until 10:00 p.m., waiting for them to get home from shopping because it was the last day to sign for month end, and the Almighty Quota had to be met. Signing a day later and funding the loan the first of the next month was unacceptable.

My purpose in sharing this story is that when a loan officer suggests that you refinance, it doesn't necessarily mean it's in your best interest to do so. There might be something else going on behind the scenes. You must take responsibility for making a smart decision yourself, and you must look at the fees.

One day, I went out on a house call with a loan officer meeting with a homeowner, just to observe. The loan officer said, "Most loans have five or six points, but I'm just charging three, so I'm giving you a good deal."

"Thank you," said the homeowner.

"You're welcome. I'll need your signature right here on this Good Faith Estimate," she said as she slid her pen down the page. "This $995 is just our customary junk fee, and the other fees go to the appraiser, title, escrow, recording, et cetera. Sign and date at the bottom, here."

The homeowner signed, never questioning why the loan officer called the administration fee junk or whether three points was too much to pay, compared with her monthly savings.

👎 Bad Practice

Ignoring the closing costs just because they're covered by your loan and not out of pocket.

👍 Good Practice

Choosing your refinance as carefully—at least—as you choose your original loan.

How Much Will It Cost You to Save Money?

It's easy to subtract your proposed monthly payment from your current monthly payment. That is a good first step to see how much money you'll save in monthly outgo.

But then add up the actual loan fees—excluding property taxes, homeowners' insurance, and prepaid interest. You don't count taxes, insurance, and prepaid interest because those are not loan fees, and they'll end up being "a wash" anyway.

(Prepaid interest is paying for the exact number of days from the time your loan closes to the end of the month. If you close on June 15, there will be 15 days of prepaid interest because you have your new loan from June 16–30. And then your old loan stops on June 15, so it's exactly fair. The first payment on your new loan will be August 1, skipping July, because mortgage payments are made in arrears.)

Let's say your refinance will save you $200 per month. Let's say the loan Origination Fee, lender fees, and third-party fees equal $5,000 (not counting taxes, insurance, or prepaid interest). Divide the cost by the savings to see how many months it will take for you to break even.

$5,000 ÷ $200 = 25 months (Just slightly more than two years.)

Now you know if you keep the loan more than two years, you'll come out ahead by refinancing. Because you plan to stay in your home at least five years and maybe more, that's good. But wait, we're not done yet. Let's go back and consider the other questions.

How far are you into your loan now? Let's say you bought your house three years ago. Because you've got 27 years left, it's not a giant setback to go to 30 years again. Keep in mind that if you make one extra principle-and-interest payment per year, you'll shave that down to about 23 years, so the prospect of refinancing is looking good.

Skipping Ahead to Save Money

On the other hand, let's say you bought your house 12 years ago and you plan to stay there forever. In that case, you'd want to consider a 15-year loan. That would get you to your goal of total home ownership faster as you would be jumping ahead three years rather than going backward by 12. If you're in sight of retiring, that could be an important consideration. It's preferable not to have a mortgage during the retirement years.

Getting Out of an Adjustable Rate or an Interest Only Loan

Let's take another scenario. You have a 5/1 ARM that is going to adjust next year. Your current rate is 4.5 percent, so next year it will go to 6.5 percent. Right now, you could refinance into 5 percent. Should you do it? If you're going to keep your house for more than two years, I say yes. If you're going to sell within two years, I say no.

Reaching a Conclusion

By looking at some simple numbers and then asking yourself the other questions, I believe you can make a wise choice in refinancing or not. Yes, there are other factors, such as interest you could be earning on the money saved, the difference in income tax deductions, etc., but that gets too mathematically detailed for most people—and besides, your conclusion about refinancing will probably be the same without creating a complex spreadsheet. Here's what I mean...

Some People Are So Smart, They Blow Your Mind

One afternoon, a mathematical genius asked me whether I thought we should buy expensive toner for our office printer or just buy a whole new printer that would use cheaper toner. I asked him a couple questions, thought about it for a few moments, and then said, "Let's buy a new printer. I think we'll come out ahead that way."

Well, he didn't love my answer because I made it too quickly using my gut instinct. So he went back to his desk and created a chart. He calculated how much printing we did per month, on average. He calculated the cost of ink per page, both for black and for color, and then both for our current printer and for the new printer. He calculated how many years of life were left in the current printer. He calculated the cost of each and every part we might have to replace if we kept the current printer.

For real, he spent several hours calculating a whole bunch of stuff, and when he was done, he had the fanciest chart of little numbers I ever saw. Then with an expression of sheer triumph—you'd think he'd just outswam Michael Phelps—he presented his chart to me. It was so complex, it took eight minutes to explain it all, but it was a work of mind-blowing accuracy. Then he proclaimed, loud and clear: "In conclusion, we should buy a new printer!"

"Fantastic," I said. "You did a great job of figuring it out. I respect your decision. Let's do that."

I didn't mention the fact that it was the same decision I'd come to in two minutes using my instincts.

You get my point. Look at the whole picture, check the important numbers, use common sense, and go with your gut. You don't have to go overboard factoring in every penny to figure out if refinancing is financially beneficial. By the same token, never let anyone talk you into ignoring your inner voice and refinancing so they can meet their corporate-mandated quota.

Coming Up Next

If you have a question about refinancing that hasn't been answered yet, check out the Q and A next.

23

I'm Glad You Asked: Refinancing Q and A

Random, yet important questions homeowners have asked me about refinancing are here, with my answers. Feel free to browse through these questions and read the answers for the ones that interest you. Don't skip the last question, as it is for every homeowner.

Q: "My refinance was going great until the appraisal report came in. The value assigned by the appraiser is unrealistically low. Do I have any recourse?"

A: Declined values have hit homeowners hard, and most people are surprised to learn what their current value is. However, if you truly believe the value is incorrect, follow these steps:

- Ask for a copy of the appraisal report, and then study it for accuracy. Make sure the number of rooms, age, and square footage is correct. Study the comparable homes to verify that they are good samples.
- Write out a factual list showing why your home should be assigned more value. Don't write an emotional essay; just list the facts. End with a statement that says something like, "Thank you for your consideration of these facts when taking a second look at my appraised value."
- Send the letter or e-mail to the appraiser. His or her response will be your final answer. Don't counterargue.
- If you still believe your home is grossly undervalued, you can ask your loan officer to order another appraisal from a different company; but be sure, because that means an additional appraisal fee for you.

For more information on this topic, see Chapter 29, "Home Value Rip-Offs."

Q: "Can I pay my taxes and insurance outside of the loan—and is it a good idea to do so?"

A: If you have at least 20 percent equity in your home, you may pay taxes and insurance outside of a conventional loan. However, there is a one-time fee of .25 percent. This can be paid as an extra closing cost, or you can take a higher interest rate so that there is at least .25 percent Yield Spread Premium to cover it. (On a $200,000 loan, the fee would be $500.) If your loan officer doesn't mention an extra fee for not having the taxes included in your payment, they're probably covering it with the YSP and not telling you because they think it's likely you would throw a fit and they don't want to upset you. Because this is a rule set by the Federal National Mortgage Association (Fannie Mae), there is no negotiation.

Whether to include it or not is a personal preference issue. Some people want to keep their money in an interest-bearing account and pay their own tax bill twice a year; whereas others are happy to include it in their payment so they don't have to deal with it.

For an FHA or VA loan, taxes and insurance must be included in the payment.

If you have a loan that is neither backed by Fannie Mae or Freddie Mac, you need to ask your loan officer as it can vary, per individual lender.

Q: "My loan officer says I have to pay an extra fee to get cash out on my refinance. Is that a rip-off?"

A: It's not a rip-off, it's a statistic. Years back, there was no extra fee for a cash out refinance; but then, statistics revealed more homeowners who took cash-out defaulted on their loans than those who didn't. This caused Fannie Mae to add a fee when the loan-to-value (LTV) ratio is above 60 percent to offset the risk. The fee is based on both the LTV and your credit score. Blame the deadbeat homeowners of yesteryear for the fee, not the lenders. But if you have at least 40 percent equity, there is no extra fee for cash out.

Q: "I paid for title insurance when I bought my house, so why do I have to pay for it again when I refinance?"

A: I do have some good news for you about this. When you purchased your home, you were required to obtain an owner's title policy, and you will not have to get that again. Also, you may get a reissue (discount) rate if it's been less than six years. But, you will be required to obtain a lender's policy of title insurance, naming the new lender as the insured. Since the time of your last title search, all kinds of things could have happened—anything from a tax lien to a fraudulent heir popping up to claim their "share," and title insurance provides assurance to investors that the mortgage is secure.

Q: My loan officer says I have to pay an extra fee to refinance because I have a townhome (or condominium), but I didn't have to pay extra when I bought it. What's going on?

A: As statistics about loan defaults come in, lending guidelines change. As of 2009, a fee of .75 percent (of the loan amount) is required for condos and townhomes when the loan is above 75 percent loan-to-value ratio. Just so you know, all loan officers dislike these fee add-ons they are required to charge their clients.

Q: What is a streamline refinance, and is it a good deal?

A: The FHA streamline refinance is a great deal with no downside. If you qualify, take it and enjoy the monthly savings.

Q: Should I avoid paying off my mortgage to keep from losing my tax deduction?

A: Only if the mortgage lender is your favorite charity. Keeping a mortgage purely for the tax deduction is idiotic. Pay off your mortgage and then if you want the same tax deduction, donate the amount of money you used to pay in interest to a church, a children's mission, or other worthy charity. You'll gain the same tax deduction. Who would you rather feed: hungry orphans or fat bankers?

Coming Up Next

The next chapters are for everyone getting a mortgage, refinance, or purchase. They reveal scams, rip-offs, and ploys—information you don't want to miss!

24

Unique Loans, Unique Situations

Jerry is desperate to take advantage of the declined home prices in Arizona. Houses that were going for a quarter of a million dollars are sitting empty, being offered for less than half that amount. There are so many of these bank-owned properties for sale, some lucky investors are snatching them up well below market value. You can tell that they're priced low when multiple offers are pouring in.

Jerry smells money, and he wants to jump aboard the gravy train by purchasing a rental property. He's got enough cash to put down 50 percent. He's got a credit score over 740. He's ready to rock on, all except for one thing. He took several months off work last year to travel the country, so his W2 shows a small income, one that's too little to qualify for the mortgage. Consequently, he gets denied.

That doesn't stop Jerry. He points out that his down payment is so large, there is no risk. His credit is good, and he has no late payments. He sends photos of the houses he's considering, to wow the underwriter and show they're instant equity machines. His loan should be a no-brainer, according to him. Then to top off his arguments, he adds that he's got a collection of baseball cards that is worth close to 100 grand. Now that's some added security because if he falls on hard times, he can always sell those, he says.

The underwriter is not impressed and turns down the application again. Why? Because the debt-to-income portion is pass or fail. No compensating factors make up for lack of verifiable cash coming in to meet all obligations. Except for one loan program…

No Income Verification Loan

Yes, in some states, the Stated Income loan is still alive in a post-subprime world. You simply state your income and the lender takes your word for it with no documentation required. Through your mortgage broker, you can get this No Income Verification (NIV) loan if you have been self-employed for at least two years (proven with a business license) and if you have excellent credit and at least 25 percent down payment. But, it's only for a home you will live in as your primary residence. Absolutely no investment/rental properties can be financed without proving your income. Sorry, no exceptions—even if you have the world's finest baseball card collection. Sadly, Jerry gets left off the gravy train.

Some people are outraged by the NIV loan. They rant about lenders giving loans to people who can't document enough income. But I disagree with this attitude. It's a narrow viewpoint that shows a lack of experience in the lending arena. For example, I had a client, a widow, who had insufficient income for her debt ratio to qualify; but her husband left her over a million dollars in assets and her credit score was 800. She could pay cash, but her financial advisor said it would be more advantageous for her to take a mortgage. Why shouldn't she be allowed to take a NIV loan? I could cite other examples of equally worthy clients with make-sense situations for the NIV loan.

Yes, there were liars who took advantage, but this is a valid loan. I hope more lenders will reinstate it in the future for good folks who can honestly benefit from this program.

If you take a NIV loan, be prepared to pay a higher loan Origination Fee and take a higher interest rate as well. Your mortgage broker can quote you pricing for your state and situation.

Home Equity Line of Credit (HELOC)

Need some quick cash? Borrow from yourself by opening up a Home Equity Line of Credit, secured on your property. That's the lure. But should you take the bait?

To explain, a Home Equity Line of Credit (HELOC) is a loan secured on your property. Some lenders allow up to 75 percent combined loan-to-value, based on both your first mortgage and HELOC. If you have a good credit score and the equity, it's an easy loan to get. Only a limited amount of paperwork is required, and a full appraisal is not needed. Some banks and credit unions offer it so cheap, it's like a grocery store's loss leader to get you in the door. It's the bait to gain you as a customer, and then they want you to switch all your banking needs to their institution.

Let's say your HELOC is $50,000. You decide how much cash you want to take out right away. You may take the entire $50,000; or you may take just $10,000; or you may take zero. You receive something like a checkbook. You then write checks for additional money and can draw out up to your $50,000 limit. Each month, your bill is calculated on your current balance and the current interest rate. If there's no balance, no payment is due.

A prepayment penalty might apply, so look for the terms. A small prepay, such as $300, is not a stopper if the HELOC will provide a bigger benefit to you. The same goes for an annual fee.

One young couple asked me if it would be a good idea to open up a HELOC so they'd have it in case of emergency—such as if they lost their jobs and needed to use it while their house was up for sale. I have loan officer friends who have HELOCs with zero balances, waiting as safety nets in case they need them. They figured they'd get one while they were still employed and could. The annual fee was considered cheap insurance. If a person has the self-discipline to leave the HELOC alone and can resist the temptation to fund granite countertops and other luxuries, I am not opposed.

Some people take a HELOC to consolidate credit cards or buy an auto or fund their anniversary cruise. I am opposed to all of those uses of a HELOC. That is what you call using your home as a piggy bank, and it's the first step to what can be a slippery slope to debt hell.

Furthermore, when you've taken out a HELOC after the original sale of your home, your refinance will be considered a "cash out" refinance and have an extra fee. That's tripped up many homeowners from being able to refinance into a lower rate and payment.

Second Home or Vacation Home

Live like a celebrity by vacationing in a beachside condo or cozy cabin that you own. Go on extended family getaways without breaking the bank when you say adieu to high-priced hotels. Does that sound like a lifestyle you'd enjoy? If so, owning a second home might be for you.

You'll need a down payment of 5 percent to 20 percent down, and you'll get the same interest rate as for your primary residence (unlike a rental property, which is priced higher).

The main caveat is that you have to qualify for the payment on both homes. When constructing your personal budget, remember to include maintenance, taxes, and Homeowners Association (HOA) dues, if applicable. Watch out for the IRS who wants a piece of everything it can get. According to current rules, if you rent out your vacation home for more than 14 days a year, you must pay taxes on the net rental income after expenses. Consult with your tax attorney about which tax bracket that might put you into and about updated IRS rules.

Duplex or Multiplex Property

Because this type of property carries additional risk, an additional cost is charged. You may cover this by an up-front fee or by taking a higher interest rate. Your loan officer can give you the current fees and rates.

Condominium or Townhome

In 2009, the Federal National Mortgage Association (Fannie Mae) set a new rule for financing condos and townhomes that are specified as condominiums on title. Any loan over 75 percent loan-to-value ratio (less than 25 percent down payment or 25 percent equity) has an additional cost. It may be paid by an up-front fee of .75 percent (of the loan amount), or by taking a higher interest rate (which will vary day to day, so check with your loan officer).

Kiddie Condo Loan

A good way for parents to help their young adult kids get started buying their first home is with the FHA Kiddie Condo Loan Program. Parent and child are coborrowers on the loan and coowners on title, so the parent's income and assets help the child qualify. But everyone must have the credit rating to qualify (620 score with no late payments in the last 12 months preferred).

Here are four pluses of the Kiddie Condo Loan:

1. Only 3.5 percent down payment (versus 20 percent on an investment property).
2. Get a lower interest rate because it's considered owner occupied, not a rental.
3. The young adult gets a leg up in boosting his or her credit rating.
4. It's okay to rent out a bedroom to another person, which helps cover the cost of the mortgage payment.

Now here's the topper for all this good news: The property does not have to be a condo. You can use this program with a single family house as well.

Reverse Mortgage for Seniors

I have a neighbor, in her eighties, who has been receiving a check for $1,000 each and every month for the past 15 years, courtesy of her house. This additional income, from a reverse mortgage, has enabled her to live comfortably. Here's how it works.

A "reverse" mortgage is a loan that pays you, rather than you paying into it; hence, the reverse feature. You can receive either a lump sum, monthly payments, or a combination of the two. Or, you can choose to set up a credit line, which can be handy for emergencies, personal use, or even to buy a vacation home.

If you choose monthly payments, the checks will never stop, guaranteed, as long as you live in your home. No need to worry about outliving your equity. It doesn't matter; you still receive the money every month. In a scenario like that, the bank loses. But don't worry too much about that; the bank makes enough money on its other reverse mortgages to come out ahead—just as insurance companies will lose money on a few customers, but come out ahead overall.

What's the catch? Along with the money you receive, there is a profit built in for the bank, in the form of a low interest rate. It's usually an adjustable rate based on either the U.S. Treasury (T-Bill) or the LIBOR index (London InterBank Offered Rate). Both your monthly check and the bank's profit are subtracted from your equity. When you sell the home, move out, or upon your passing, the amount owed is subtracted from the profit you or your heirs will receive.

The other "catch" is that there are up-front fees and closing costs, which are also deducted from your future equity. Typically, you don't pay for any fees or costs out of pocket, except for the appraisal and the required housing counseling (your loan officer will set you up with). Costs can vary between lenders, so I suggest you compare three before you decide.

Is a reverse mortgage a good deal? If you plan to stay in your home a long time, a reverse mortgage can be more than just a good deal—it can be a godsend. In addition to providing you with money to live on, it pays off your existing mortgage and can be used to get much-needed repairs done on your home. Let's say you are still paying your mortgage, can't afford to update your bathroom (or even fix the leaky plumbing), and are barely getting by with enough money for groceries. A reverse mortgage gets rid of your mortgage payments, fixes your bathroom, and pays you additional cash every month. How could that not be a good deal, if you want to remain in your home for a long time?

Just don't get a reverse mortgage if you plan to sell and move into an assisted living community within two years, because the up-front fees are too high to be worth it for the short-term.

What about my children? Yes, what about them? They're adults, right? They should be making their own way in the world. This is *your* house that you've spent years of *your* life to acquire; so, in my opinion, the equity belongs to *you* to enjoy a nice life with in your golden years. Only a selfish, self-centered child would want his parent to struggle so he could pocket more cash in an inheritance, and I'm sure that wouldn't be *your* child.

Don't worry if there's negative equity by the time you pass on because with a reverse mortgage, no one ever has to pay the bank, even if the equity ran out long ago. But most often, there is equity remaining. Your heirs can then choose to convert the reverse mortgage into a traditional mortgage to keep the house, or they can sell the home so both they and the bank get paid.

Who can qualify? All homeowners must be at least age 62, the home has to be on a permanent foundation, and there must be enough money available from the reverse mortgage to pay off any existing mortgage.

How much money can I get? That depends on the current equity in your home and your age. Again, credit scores or income have nothing to do with it. To get a specific answer to this question, speak with a loan officer who specializes in reverse mortgages, or try the online calculator at www.RMAARP.com/.

Will it affect my Social Security or Medicare? No, government programs are not affected by a reverse mortgage. On the other hand, Medicaid or other need-based programs might be affected, depending on how much you retain each month.

Do I pay taxes on the income from a reverse mortgage? No, you do not pay taxes on the money you get from your home. What's more, at the end of the term when the bank is paid, the interest paid on the reverse mortgage is tax deductible.

Is there a scam or rip-off I need to be aware of? Yes, I'm glad you asked! Wherever there's money to be made, there are shady characters lurking nearby. Some scammers—calling themselves insurance or investment professionals—convince seniors to use their reverse mortgage money to buy variable annuities, stocks, or other so-called investments that cause them to lose money. Never work with anyone who wants to bundle your reverse mortgage with another money plan because it's going to be a scheme where you will be taken advantage of.

Coming Up Next

Don't miss the twisted truth, deception à la the Better Business Bureau, the loan "they" don't want you to know about, or bogus rate quotes, coming up next.

25

Beware of Radio Ads

If you've ever been tempted to respond to a radio ad, you might change your mind after reading this. Don't get me wrong. I love the radio. I love talk shows and talk show hosts. There's nothing I like more than being invited for an on-air interview or to answer listeners' questions live on the air. But some of those radio ads are something else altogether.

Twisted Truth

There's a mortgage company down the road from me that I used to call on when I worked as an account executive for First Franklin wholesale lending. The owner of this company looked me in the eye, grinned with glee, and said he couldn't wait for his next lawsuit. His big plan was to sue every mortgage company that quoted an interest rate on the air without also quoting an APR (Annual Percentage Rate, a rate that calculates both the interest rate and some of the closing costs into one number). He sued four of his competitors.

Rather than suffer the public humiliation of their mistake, they settled outside of court and paid him a wad of cash. He then used the loot to buy a lot of airtime for himself.

Every good salesman has a "unique selling position," and his was Truth-in-Lending. According to him, that is. His ads made a big deal out of charging "no points." As if points, which unlike other fees are tax deductible, were a bad thing.

One day, off the air, a radio host asked him, "If you don't charge any points, how do you make money?"

He replied, "I charge 2 percent on every loan. It's in the fine print, and no one has ever noticed."

So much for his Truth-in-Lending ads—paid for by his chagrined competitors. And of course, the radio listeners had no way of knowing this; the ads sounded good but were deceptive.

Chosen by the Better Business Bureau— So What!

On down the road to another mortgage company—again, one I called on as an account executive. Over the course of a year, I caught them red-handed in two blatant lies and one federal violation. And yet, they advertised heavily on the radio that they were chosen by the Better Business Bureau as the company of the year. What did it take to win that honor? I believe it was donating the most money to the BBB and volunteering the most at charity events. It certainly had nothing to do with offering the cheapest loans. After all, the Better Business Bureau does not conduct an audit of the loans or interview mortgagees.

Back to the radio advertising: According to an insider, this company put $90,000 into radio ads. They had to pay for those somehow, and as someone who read enough of the GFEs to know, I can assure you it wasn't by offering the cheapest deals to their customers.

👎 Bad Practice

Responding to a radio ad just because it's aired on a Christian radio station. That doesn't mean the loan officers there are all Christians who treat you to the best pricing. Even if the ad is spoken by your favorite Christian disc jockey, it doesn't mean it's a great loan. That naive thinking is out.

The same goes for radio ads on stations that cater to the Hispanic or African-American community.

> 👍 **Good Practice**
>
> Considering a company with a good radio ad along with two other companies by reviewing their Good Faith Estimates. The ad itself should have no influence on your decision.

The Loan "They Don't Want You to Know About"

I couldn't believe my ears when I heard a radio ad that said this particular mortgage company was offering a loan that the other lenders didn't want you to know about because "they don't make any money on it." Just how naive do they think people are? A loan they don't make money on? That would be called a donation, not a loan. And, since when did the mortgage industry turn into a big, benevolent charity?

I actually called the number on the ad, and to my delight, the manager answered.

I said, "I'm in the mortgage business myself, and there is no such thing as a loan lenders don't make money on."

He replied, "You're right, but as a marketing tactic, it works."

And that was the key: "It works." People were responding to this ridiculous advertisement.

Think about this: If no one made money on the loan, why would they be paying for an ad to tell you about it?

And if no one responded to his deceptive ad, he'd stop putting it on the air.

Bogus Rate Quotes

A rate quote accompanied by an APR on the radio is as real as a Cinderella fairy tale. Why? Because rates change daily, and sometimes two or three times during the day as well. An ad is prepared and recorded in advance; therefore, by the time you hear it, it's already stale news. I'm not accusing the advertisers as being deliberately dishonest; I'm just telling you not to count on a rate quoted over the air or in a newspaper either, for that matter.

"We Give the Best Service"

Does an offer for good service really mean anything any more? Can you imagine a company saying they had so-so service or poor service? However, we all know there are plenty of companies out there with so-so and poor service.

And exactly what does "best service" mean anyway? That they'll return your phone calls and e-mails in a timely manner? That they'll give you a Good Faith Estimate, per federal law? Will they disclose their Yield Spread Premium or overage? *(Now that would be something!)* That they'll keep you informed throughout the loan process? That they'll speak in a kind and polite manner? It seems to me that all of the above should be the norm, not a standard for "best service." So again, what does their statement really mean to you? And how are they better at service than their competitors who are also prompt, thorough, professional, and nice?

If you're a loan officer and you do truly offer best service that is certifiably better than all your competitors, please send me an e-mail and tell me what it is that places you above all others. (Go to www.AskCarolynWarren.com to send me an e-mail.)

Coming Up Next

Listen up all you young computer whizzes and all you youngsters-at-heart who love the Internet. You've got to stop clicking on those Internet ads for mortgages. I tell you why, next.

26

Stop Clicking on Mortgage Ads

I came across that clever slogan on the Internet again today. I don't know exactly how much money it's brought in to the company, but an insider told me it's in the millions. I believe him. The public has been falling for the pitch like overroasted marshmallows into a campfire. I'm sure you've heard or seen it too:

"When banks compete, you win."

It's a brilliant piece of copywriting, and I wish I knew who wrote it. The big problem is that it's misleading.

Three Reasons the "Compete Slogan" Is Deceptive

We know that competition is good for consumers. Competition drives down prices. So what's wrong with "when banks compete, you win"? Why doesn't this ad make good sense for you?

1. Going through a lead generation system costs you more money.

   A lead generation company advertises to collect prospective customers, and then sells those prospects to an interested company, such as a mortgage lender. When a lead generation company gets to sell your information four times to four competing lenders, they make good money—perhaps more money than the loan officer who actually does all the work on your loan.

   According to their own marketing information, Lending Tree sells their leads for over $1200 each. This means a loan officer has to build in that much extra profit, if he wants to make the same amount of money he normally does. Guess who ends up paying for it in the end? The borrower, of course.

2. Your credit might get pulled over and over, lowering your score.

Folks have been shocked and angry to discover their credit has been pulled over and over again by multiple companies, lowering their credit score, because they unknowingly filled out the online application for a lead generation system—and I don't just mean the one with this fancy slogan. There are many lead generation companies and many lead generation Internet ads.

3. You don't get the competitive advantage you think you get.

Anytime you go to a mortgage broker, wholesale lending companies "compete." That is what a mortgage broker is all about: saving you money by shopping various wholesale banks. So there's nothing unique about signing up with a lead generation service, except that there is an additional advertising cost involved, and your name and Social Security number get sold multiple times. But make no mistake: There is no extra competing going on that will produce a lower interest rate for you.

Maybe a more accurate slogan would be, "When banks compete, the lead generation system wins."

👎 Bad Practice

Using a lead generation service to dole out your application to their own lenders—lenders who pay for your information.

👍 Good Practice

Doing your own loan shopping. When you work with a mortgage broker, wholesale lenders are competing for your business. It's automatic and organic.

Jumping Girls and Rolling Eyeballs: What's Behind Those Action Ads

They look funny, those ads popping up on your e-mail. There's a guy doing backflips and a sexy girl jumping up and down. I saw one that was really annoying though. It was a giant pair of eyes rolling at the top of my computer screen. I thought an enormous freak was staring me down. The text said click to find out how low interest rates had become.

Some Internet ads are serious, with maps of the United States where you're supposed to click on your state to see how much a house payment would be for your location. Other ads use a political headline to grab your attention. Those headlines tie in to recent economic news, like it's relevant to their promotion, when it's not. They're hoping people will see the headline, remember something they saw on TV or read in the newspaper, and then naively think that news means the interest rate is lower or mortgage money is easier to qualify for. Today, I saw an Internet ad that mentioned bailout money and then there was a box to click to "find out what your mortgage payment will be." Another one said to enter your zip code to find out what interest rate you could get. I entered mine just to see what would happen. It led me to a page where I was prompted to enter my address and other personal information; it was like a mini loan application. So the zip code/interest rate bait was just to get you hooked into their system so they could sell your information as a lead to a lending institution. With these come-ons, there's a huge disconnect between the headline and reality.

If you click one of these ads and fill out their form, you don't know who you're communicating with—it could be a horrid lead generation company that sells your information to a dozen different inexperienced loan officers, for example. Nothing good can come from clicking those ads.

Why Advertised Rates Are Phony

The ads that post a certain mortgage rate are also meaningless. Because interest rates change a minimum of once a day, posting an Internet ad with an interest rate and APR (Annual Percentage Rate) is as meaningful as posting last month's gasoline price.

One day, I decided to test an advertised rate that seemed to be too good to be true. It wasn't a pop-up ad; it was a rate posted on a mortgage Web site that was half a percent lower than what I could get as a mortgage broker myself. I wondered, which lender has a 30-year fixed rate that low? I called and asked to speak with the manager. Sure enough, the interest rate came with extra buy-down points.

The same thing goes for newspaper and radio ads. Any advertised interest rate is to be taken with a grain of salt. Assume it is a general ballpark figure and could vary by three-quarters of a percent, either way. In between writing the ad and having it printed or aired, the rates could have changed several times.

There's just no point in advertising a specific rate—unless it's a bogus come-on just to get people to call.

👎 Bad Practice

Finding a lender through Internet ads.

👍 Good Practice

Finding a lender through reputation. That could be through a personal referral, through a book, or through a loan officer's actual Web site.

Coming Up Next

Favorite tricks and snares banks love to use to lure homebuyers into their doors and trap them are coming up next.

27

Deception Exposed

Some ideas might sound good, but a closer look reveals the pitfalls. For example, it's been proven time after time that the word *free* is a lure most people can't resist. It's amazing how expensive some of those free offers turn out to be! One common lure used in the mortgage business is the so-called free appraisal report. Let's take a closer look at that and other ploys.

"Free" Appraisal Report

Appraisers do not work for free. If you get that marketing come-on by a lender, just know you are paying for the appraisal in another way—either through a fee called by another name or through the Yield Spread Premium or overage, which means you took a higher interest rate to cover it.

If a loan officer says, "We pay for your appraisal report," you can smile knowingly and say something like, "Please, don't insult my intelligence. I would prefer it if you were transparent in your charge for the appraisal rather than bury it in another fee or the Yield Spread Premium or Service Release Premium. Don't you think that advertising ploy is a little outdated? Nowadays, people read and research, and we are not naive about financing." Then sit back and watch their eyes grow big like a Tweety Bird.

One loan officer told me they advertise "no cost for the appraisal," but they cover it by a $700 fee called "other." One of my book readers tried asking what the "other" fee was for, and the banker said, "It's just the standard stuff that goes into a loan." Like that explained anything!

I spotted an ad in a coupon book placed by a Realtor that said she paid for your appraisal report. That is believable because the Realtor worked in an upscale neighborhood; so if she earns 3 percent on the sale of a $500,000 home, she can realistically afford to reimburse you for the $400 appraisal report. However, a Realtor is not allowed to kick in for your closing costs on the HUD-1 Settlement Statement, so that offer has to be taken care of outside the loan itself.

No Points

A point is 1 percentage point of the loan amount. It might be called an Origination Fee, Broker Fee, or Discount Fee. You have a choice of paying a point or more—or of paying no points and taking a higher interest rate instead.

What I don't like is the big advertising banner that says, "No points!" As if paying points is a bad thing or something that should be avoided. First, the points can be an income tax deduction. Check with your CPA for tax advice, but typically, on a purchase loan, you can deduct all points in the first year; and on a refinance, the points are spread out over the number of years in the loan. Remember Leanne's advantageous strategy in Chapter 1, "Getting the World's Cheapest Loan"?

In our current market, investors are highly in favor of the borrower paying a point. Why? Because it means the borrower is putting something in and won't be as likely to skip out after a couple of months. When a lender doesn't get to keep a loan for at least six months, they lose money.

Right now, we're seeing that it makes sense to pay a point and take a significantly lower interest rate. In times past, paying a point might have gotten you a rate that was .25 percent better. Today, a point might get you a rate of .75 better. The monthly savings you gain by paying the percentage point is quickly assimilated so you come out financially ahead in the long run. Even still, there are loan officers flaunting the "no point" banner like it's a big advantage to one and all. To decide, you have to calculate your payment both ways and see how much you save. Then divide the savings into the cost. This will tell you how many months it takes to recover the cost—and *voila!* You can make an intelligent decision.

Let's look at an example:

Calculate the Cost of Paying a Percentage Point

$300,000 loan @ 5.75% with 0 points = $1,750 mo. P&I

$300,000 loan @ 5.0% with 1 point = $1,610 mo. P&I

Difference (savings) = $140/mo.

1 percentage point on $300,000 = $3,000 (cost)

$3,000 ÷ $140 = 21.4 months to recover the cost

Less than two years to recover the cost of paying the percentage point—not bad! Now do the same for your own scenario, and the choice will be clear.

No-Cost Mortgage

"Zero-cost" mortgage, "no-cost" mortgage! That sounds kind of like free money. What could possibly be wrong with that?

Interestingly, today I read a post on a forum for mortgage professionals that said, "I put my borrower into a no-cost loan so that I could refinance him again in a few months."

Did you catch that? The purpose of the no-cost loan was so that the loan officer would have repeat business shortly. Was it in the borrower's best interest? No. It was all about collecting another commission check. I'll explain.

Let's assume that it is a true no-cost loan and not a sneaky bait and switch where they tell you it's no cost, but then you discover they "didn't count" certain fees. That's bogus—if anyone ever does that to you, just say "No thank you" and walk away. But let's say it is a true no-cost loan with no lender fees (Origination Fee, Broker Fee, underwriting fee, administration fee, application fee, processing fee) and no third-party fees (credit report, appraisal, escrow, attorney, title, recording).

First, the lender is going to require a higher interest rate to make up for the lost revenue of up-front fees. And second, someone has to pay all those third-party bills—and if it's the lender, then they're going to require an *even higher* interest rate to get a Yield Spread Premium or overage to cover those bills. So you get the picture: With a no-cost loan, you take a significantly higher interest rate to cover all the costs you didn't pay for up front.

Now you see how that loan officer who posted on the forum was setting up his borrower to refinance. First, he does the "no-cost" thing, and then because he doesn't have the lowest interest rate, he refinances again six months later. Good for the loan officer, but silly for the homeowner because he has to start over with "month one" of the 360-month loan again. Remember, in the first month, your payment goes almost entirely to interest, with each month decreasing a little. The chart looks like an upside-down pyramid. You don't want to start over at the broad top again and again and again because you don't get ahead financially that way.

Speaking of getting financially ahead, a lot of folks are asking about equity acceleration.

👎 Bad Practice

Serial refinancing.

👍 Good Practice

Getting a great loan from the get-go so you don't need to refinance; or if rates improve so that refinancing makes sense, aim to do so only once.

Equity Acceleration Programs

If you've read this far, you know I'm all for paying off your mortgage and owning your home free and clear. However, I am against smoke-and-mirrors presentations that lead people to believe they'll save money with a certain method or system when it is not true.

There are pricey software programs that guide you through your monthly finances. One sells for about $3,500. Supposedly, you get a clever secret unbeknown to North America until recently. That's laughable! In actuality, it's nothing more than a commonsense financial plan and a handy Web site to track your money. The reason it's so expensive is because it is a multilevel marketing (MLM) company. (The most famous MLM is Amway.) When there are all those levels of sales representatives to pay, the product has to be overpriced. But that's not all. There's the catch—and it's a big one.

Several of these so-called equity builder/acceleration programs guide you to open a Home Equity Line of Credit (HELOC) and run all your money through it. They claim "you're using the bank's money to pay off your mortgage faster." I thought that sounded good, so I signed up as an agent, paid the fee, and took the 100-question test to make it official. This gave me access to the software, and I spent a week running all types of scenarios through the program. I had the help of a computer engineer at the University of Washington to analyze the results. Our finding?

There is absolutely no advantage whatsoever to funneling your money through a HELOC to pay off your mortgage. You do not pay off your mortgage any faster that way than if you paid the extra on your principal balance yourself. In fact, you will take about three months longer due to the cost of the software rolled into the HELOC and the small amount of interest that goes toward the HELOC. When you tell this to one of the sales reps, they get red in the face and jump up and down like savages about to lose their last meal. I've heard them shout and swear and proclaim that it's not true, and that anyone who says their program doesn't save you money is a moron. Why all the emotion? Because, according to their own marketing materials and testimonials, the sales reps can rake in $20,000 and more per month when they get a pyramid of other sales reps under them.

There are two disadvantages of this system you should be aware of:

1. When you open a HELOC and carry a balance, if you ever want to refinance, it will be considered a "cash out refinance" and have an extra cost if the loan-to-value ratio is above 60 percent. That alone has prevented homeowners from taking advantage of lower interest rates, and it's a shame.

2. Having an open, available HELOC is a financial death trap for some people who can't resist the temptation to use the available money for home improvements and other desires. They then end up in a worse financial position than before they began.

Fancy colorful charts showing how many years you cut off your mortgage and how much wealth you'll accumulate by investing that money instead are delightful; but why pay thousands of dollars for something you can do on your own? Or with a software program that sells for less than $50? Why pay commissions on a pyramid MLM product?

One of the reasons these programs appear to work is that they advise you to drain all of your reserve money, your financial safety net, and the cash you have in various savings and bank accounts and put all of it toward your mortgage balance immediately. Their rationale is that because you open a Home Equity Line of Credit, you have that loan available to use as a safety net and don't need your liquid cash. If you are financially savvy, you see the pitfall. First, taking cash out of your HELOC for an emergency means you'll be paying interest on it; and second, a bank can lower the amount of available cash you can get from your HELOC, thereby removing your safety net. And banks have been doing exactly that because of declining home values.

Interestingly, when I mentioned my writing this book to one of the sales reps for the equity acceleration program that was featured on the cover of *Broker-Banker* magazine, she said, "Do we really need more fear and anger in this world? Why can't you write a mortgage book that is filled only with upliftment [her word] and hope?"

And that right there is the problem: These super expensive equity acceleration programs sell by preying on your desire for hope and ignoring or even denying the scary pitfalls. I'll be thrilled to write a mortgage book without anything negative in it just as soon as everyone stops trying to get their greedy little hands into homebuyers' wallets and homeowners' equity, so that all the deception and rip-offs cease and desist.

Coming Up Next

How do certain loan officers make more money off customers with good credit than the sharks made on ugly-as-Frankenstein sub-prime loans? One mortgage trainer says it's as easy as shooting fish in a barrel. If you don't want to be one of those "fish," read what's next.

28

Watch Out for the Ten-Million-Dollar Mortgage Man (and His Cohorts)

The headline was irresistible, the same way watching a bus careen off a winding mountaintop road is irresistible. You know it's a disaster; and yet, you can't seem to tear your eyes away. I had to read on.

The headline said a particular mortgage guru brings in over $10,000,000.00 in fees, using a "forgotten system."

The subhead was even better. It went on to ask "frustrated loan officers" if they didn't want to learn how to take an "unfair advantage" over the competition.

This guru claims that he and his cohorts are making $10,000 to $20,000 fee deals as steady as clockwork. And the best part is that it seems anyone can use his method to make the big bucks because, as he wrote, it's "as easy as shooting fish in a barrel."

Now, let me ask you this: How would you like to be one of those fish in a barrel waiting to be shot? If you feel like I think you do, please read on because I'm going to tell you how to swim out of their insidious trap.

By the way, in case you think this is one whopping exaggeration, there are testimonies, accompanied by photos, names, and cities of the protégés who have also made their fortunes charging exorbitant fees to these fish in a barrel. (If you'd like to see the document, send me an e-mail from my Web site, www.AskCarolynWarren.com.)

An individual named Scott said he used to make an average of $3,000 per loan, but now he's just closed 19 deals ranging in commission from $11,000 to $16,995 each. That's a 466 percent increase!

Then, he adds that with the "right client," he could snag $25,000. By his story is a photo of a yellow Ferrari he says he accidentally bought on eBay for 30 grand. Lucky for the seller, he had the cash to make good on his bid—thanks to the fish in a barrel.

Reading on, I discovered that Scott's dream of making $25,000 on a single customer is not unrealistic. Another success story accompanied by a photo and city/state of a particular Mr. Lee said he just closed a $817,000 loan at more than three points for a fee of $24,977.28—just two dollars and some change away from $25,000. He goes on to thank the mortgage guru for teaching him his system, on behalf of his loved ones whom he provides for.

Let me get that straight. Mr. Lee's family is grateful that he learned how to take advantage of naive, vulnerable clients and, therefore, hurt those people's families? I'm sorry, but that rubs me the wrong way.

The good news is that the real estate agents can relax. The mortgage guru says he'd rather stick a pencil in his neck than work with a Realtor. I imagine that's because if he ever tried one of his tricks on a real estate agent's clients, the agent would stick something more deadly than a pencil in his neck first. He doesn't work with accountants, financial planners, or attorneys either. Hmm, I wonder why.

👎 Bad Practice

Buying into a program to pay off your mortgage faster based on a flashy presentation.

👍 Good Practice

Consulting with two impartial CPAs or certified financial planners to protect yourself. Avoid emotional, impulsive financial decisions.

So, what is this all about? Well, first, I have to tell you that I didn't pay $4,997 to attend his seminar. But from reading his 16-page tome, it's clear that he sells his customers a total "financial plan" to get out of debt fast. His fish in a barrel are not primarily subprime borrowers, as you might suppose, but people with 720+ credit scores and a good amount of equity in their property. As all smart people with good credit do, they desire to be mortgage-free—and he's got just the ticket to get them there.

Meanwhile, back at the mansion, he's selling his system to greedy loan officers who put up five grand (minus $3) to learn his secrets. He only accepts one professional per geographic region, so with that contrived scarcity, he can pump up the price. But what does this mean to you? You need to beware because there is likely to be a clone in your area.

Be careful of smoke-and-mirrors presentations, my friends, be very careful.

Debt Today, Gone Tomorrow

One dangerous strategy that is popular with these high-priced gurus is the so-called "turn your bad debt into good debt" plan. It could be called by various names, depending on the presenter. But first, they show you how you're wasting your after-tax dollars on non-tax-deductible interest for credit cards and auto loans. Then they show you how much money you're paying in interest on your mortgage and how the total payment on a 30-year loan is about three times what you paid for the house. They add up all that money you're throwing down the drain and display it on a big chart that gets your head spinning. How could you be wasting so much of your hard-earned cash? And what could you be doing with that cash if you had it at your disposal? Perhaps you could be enjoying Hawaiian vacations with your family, like the guru, who then whets your leisure appetite by projecting on the screen a few photos of himself and his beautifully bronzed wife sunning, surfing, and hiking.

This is the segue to their so-called brilliant solution, their System, as they call it.

Refinance into a 2 percent interest rate. Roll all of your debt—auto loans, installment loans, credit cards, your mortgage, what-have-you—into a fantastically low, low payment. How much money will that save you each month? Perhaps $400 to $2,000, depending on your situation.

Now take that extra cash and invest it at 7 percent. Look at the next chart, which shows the fantastic gains you get. Aha, instead of losing money, now you're gaining money! You've "turned bad debt into good debt."

Then at some point, they show you how to pull out that money with its earnings and pay off your mortgage. Eureka—you are mortgage-free in a fraction of the time you would be on your current 30-year plan!

All the numbers and charts are right there in front of you, bigger than life. It makes so much sense, seemingly.

Then to top it off, the guru tells you a story about himself or someone he knows who was burdened with a ton of debt. He worked 60 hours a week to barely get by, not even having a minute to enjoy the fruit of his labor. He worked like a rat on a treadmill and all of his money went down the toilet to interest and to evil creditors. He knew if he didn't change his course, he would die early of a heart attack and leave his children fatherless. The drama is bigger than *The Young and the Restless*.

Then came his financial salvation! He plugged into the System—and now just five years later, he is living the dream. He owns his home free and clear and he enjoys yachting with his family and exploring beaches in the South Pacific. Wouldn't you like to follow in his footsteps?

Your emotional hot buttons are hit hard, and after seeing those number charts, you're convinced. You can't wait to sign the paperwork, which gives the guru one whopper of a commission check, multiplied by the number of folks at the seminar signing up. No wonder he paid off his mortgage faster!

But hold on. What's the catch?

Sadly, as it turns out, far too many of these eager-to-be-debt-free folks ended up losing their homes altogether. This is no exaggeration. From 2008 to present, there has been a tsunami of foreclosures due to this magical loan, the Option ARM (adjustable rate mortgage), also called the pick-a-payment loan. Here's how it works.

At first, you have the option of paying only 2 percent (or other low rate). However, mortgage interest rates are not that low, so you are actually being charged more. You get to pay 2 percent now and owe the rest for later. So while you enjoy a tiny monthly payment, the rest of what you owe is getting tacked on to your principal balance. Each and every month, the balance of what you owe grows bigger and bigger and bigger.

Then at some point, which is stated in your contract, the initial low option ends, and you have to pay the entire interest due. But now here's the rub: This new, higher interest rate is now calculated on a larger balance because you've been deferring part of your payment until later. This is called negative amortization, and it is responsible for billions of dollars of loans going bad.

When things didn't work out as they'd hoped, homeowners discovered they were upside down in what they owed and what their property was worth. They were stuck. They couldn't refinance because there was negative equity. They couldn't sell without bringing in tens of thousands of dollars to closing. And they could no longer afford their payment because it had just tripled. Tearfully, they walked out on the street, leaving their homes—and many times, a lot of furniture also—behind.

Meanwhile, back at the guru's mansion, I imagine he's enjoying the new movie theater he's just installed, complete with reclining leather chairs and a full bar for entertaining his friends, all paid for with cash, thanks to those "fish in a barrel" and the eager-beaver loan officers who paid to learn his System.

Coming Up Next

The Home Value Code of Conduct is a wolf in sheep's clothing. Read how it could cost you thousands of dollars and what recourse you have, next.

29

Home Value Rip-Offs

Thanks to unscrupulous loan officers who coerced, threatened, and bribed appraisers' to hit a certain, desired home value; on May 1, 2009, a new law called the Home Value Code of Conduct (HVCC) was inflicted upon the mortgage industry—and it has made matters worse for homeowners. In fact, HVCC has made matters worse for everyone except the big, unregulated appraisal management companies and big lenders who own a piece of the appraisal management companies—who are now gleefully raking in more cash because of it.

Get a load of this: Brokers, loan officers, loan processors, or anyone else who earns income from the close of a loan are gagged and bound, as follows:

- They may not select a specific appraiser.

    This means they cannot order an appraisal report from an appraiser who has proven himself or herself over the last 20+ years to be thorough, accurate, and fair in preparing an appraisal and calculating home value. And it means that these good appraisers who have spent a lifetime building their careers through established quality work and relationships have had their personal Rolodex of business—their livelihood—ripped away from them overnight.

    For you, the homebuyer or homeowner, it means you cannot rely on your experienced loan officers' good judgment to choose a competent appraiser. Now with HVCC, you are a victim stuck with the luck of the draw. Experienced appraisers are now replaced by a rookie or sloppy appraiser or out-of-area appraiser whose name happens to pop up on the random-order selection by a clerk at some so-called appraisal order desk.

- They may not speak to, ask about, question, or communicate in any way with the appraiser about the property value.

Like cowboys in the Wild West who got away with most anything, appraisers are now demigods who can destroy a family's financial dreams with a couple of keyboard punches. With loan officers, brokers, real estate agents, and other professionals out of the way, the natural checks-and-balance system has been destroyed. If the appraiser makes a mistake; if the appraiser uses old comparables rather than recent, more accurate ones; if the appraiser improperly uses a property across a major arterial in a worse neighborhood for comparison; if the appraiser fails to give any value whatsoever to the panoramic view that adds real value to a property; if the appraiser is too lazy to actually drive by the comparable properties and instead drags photos off the Internet that are deceptive photos; or commits any one of a dozen other blunders… the loan officer can't defend you. The loan officer is gagged and can't say a peep—all due to the new HVCC law.

If this happens to you, as a home seller or a homeowner refinancing, it could cost you thousands or even tens of thousands of dollars. Let's look at what happened to one innocent homeowner in California a few days after HVCC was sprung into law. The loan officer asked two competent, honest, and local appraisers he had done business with for many years to give him an approximate range of value for a certain address just to test how HVCC was going to work out. He did not indicate any expected value with the query, so as not to influence. He made a note of the two opinions. Then shortly, he received the appraisal report, which a clerk from his company randomly ordered, per the Home Value Code of Conduct law. He got the shock of his career.

The HVCC appraisal was $100,000 less than the bottom of the value range given by the two competent, honest, local appraisers. The comparable properties used to calculate this lowball value were from different, inferior neighborhoods. And we all know how location is key in factoring value. The appraiser chosen per HVCC was from 60 miles away and was unfamiliar with sales in the area of the subject property.

Then to add insult to injury, the lender/appraisal management service charged the homeowner $435, even though the individual appraiser charged $325. The fee was padded by $110 for this rotten report. And now because of the inaccurately low value, the home-owner could not refinance out of his interest only adjustable rate mortgage into a lower fixed rate; and according to the loan officer, will likely face problems. If this home goes into foreclosure, it becomes another vacant, bank-owned property that could sell for undervalue and, thus, hurt all the neighbors who will then face financial loss when trying to sell or refinance. One bad law, one bad appraisal, many victims.

👎 **Bad Practice**

Coercing an appraiser to value a property higher than its actual market value.

👍 **Good Practice**

Getting an accurate appraisal report. Hopefully, you won't be victim to an inaccurate lowball value due to HVCC.

It Could Happen to You

This is one story out of many, and it could happen to you. A loan officer in North Carolina reports that appraisers from 150 miles away are being sent to neighborhoods they are ill acquainted with, causing inaccurate devaluation of property. This is the tip of the proverbial iceberg.

A loan officer in New York received an appraisal report back for a refinance when it was a purchase transaction. Due to HVCC, it took three weeks to get the corrected appraisal report back, and by then the interest rate lock expired and the homeowners lost out. She called it "horrific."

One particular valuation company amassed over 800 appraisal disputes in just one month due to bad comparables, missing forms, improperly filled-out forms, and so on. The company rep. called it "a nightmare" as each dispute represents one homeowner or home-buyer who suffers having the loan process messed up as a result.

The Home Value Code of Conduct has a nice-sounding name, but it has crippled your loan officer from being able to protect you by choosing a competent, experienced appraiser for your property.

Therefore, I recommend homeowners who are refinancing or selling ask a few questions right up front when the appraiser calls to set the appointment—questions such as the following:

- How long have you had your license? (Assuming they have one, of course.)
- Where is your office?
- What city/neighborhoods did you do most of your business in before HVCC?
- Will you drive by the comparable properties yourself and take your own photographs?

If you're not satisfied with the answers you receive, refuse to set the appointment and instead call your loan officer and request another order be placed for a different appraiser. Prevention is the best remedy.

Read HVCC

You can read the code of conduct for yourself at http://www.fanniemae.com/media/pdf/030308_agreement.pdf. (See pages 9–12.)

Coming Up Next

Final thoughts and wrap-up are coming up next.

30

Final Thoughts

Although we all hate deception, overcharges, and rip-offs, I can't end this book without adding a word of caution. No good can come from treating your loan officer like a crook who's about to get caught. If you feel that way, then that loan officer is not the right match for you. Once you've found your mortgage star—a loan officer who is ethical and who works as your advocate—you can relax. You don't need to check up on them every day, driving them crazy like a kid on a road trip who says, "Are we there yet," every few miles.

In their zealous desire to get good financing, some people go overboard and make a royal nuisance of themselves, which leads the loan officer to charge them more for the extra time and grief they're causing. I wouldn't want that to happen to you.

While I was writing this book, I was also working as a loan officer. I didn't want to be cloistered away, writing, without also being down in the trenches, helping good folks buy a home or refinance their existing mortgage. I had to be in the thick of the battles going on in processing and underwriting, I had to know what interest rates were doing on a daily basis, I had to experience the angst people were going through to get approved now, in a post-subprime, credit-challenged, super strict environment. I would not consider myself fit to write about the world of mortgages without being in the thick of it. I would hope that sentiment strikes a chord with homebuyers. Do you want to read about mortgages from someone who's never been behind closed doors talking with the underwriters about getting a loan approved, who's never argued over the value of a property, who's never helped someone clean up their credit report? I would think not. And I did my best to keep the information fresh and current.

Leanne's story in the first chapter is all true, except that it is a composite of several people's experiences. All other stories are true and accurate exactly as they are, with only the names being changed to protect privacy. I share them with the hope of helping others.

Without doubt, the majority of the ugly loans have withered away like dried-up dandelions. In my first book, *Mortgage Rip-Offs and Money Savers: An Industry Insider Explains How to Save Thousands on Your Mortgage or Refinance*, I revealed the underbelly of the mortgage business to the public. I am grateful that so many readers from all around the country have written to express their appreciation for having insider information that wasn't available to them before.

But the need for ongoing education and insider information prompted me to write this book.

One thing you can count on about the mortgage industry is that the rules and guidelines will change. It is an ever-evolving business. For updates, please visit my Web sites, www.AskCarolynWarren.com and www.MortgageHelper.com. If you have a quick question that wasn't answered in this book, you're invited to send me an e-mail via my Web site, www.AskCarolynWarren.com. I will reply to you.

Thank you for taking the time to read this book, and may God guide you and bless you.

A Note from the Publisher

If you believe the information Carolyn Warren has shared in this book is valuable, if you believe more people need to know how to avoid the pitfalls that cost them hard-earned money, if you believe the good citizens of our country have the power to clean up the dirty side of the mortgage industry—*organically*—by saying no to junk fees, marketing ploys, and deceptive pricing, then please help make our country a better place by doing the following:

- Tell your friends and family about this book.
- Call or e-mail your favorite radio host and ask to have Carolyn Warren as a guest on their show.

- E-mail your local newspaper and suggest they write a review of the book.
- Recommend it in your blog.
- Suggest to the real estate agents you know that they pick up a copy for themselves. (They'll love Chapter 20, "Why You Need Agent Representation.")
- Give copies as a gift.

INDEX

D

FT Press

FINANCIAL TIMES

In an increasingly competitive world, it is quality of thinking that gives an edge—an idea that opens new doors, a technique that solves a problem, or an insight that simply helps make sense of it all.

We work with leading authors in the various arenas of business and finance to bring cutting-edge thinking and best-learning practices to a global market.

It is our goal to create world-class print publications and electronic products that give readers knowledge and understanding that can then be applied, whether studying or at work.

To find out more about our business products, you can visit us at www.ftpress.com.